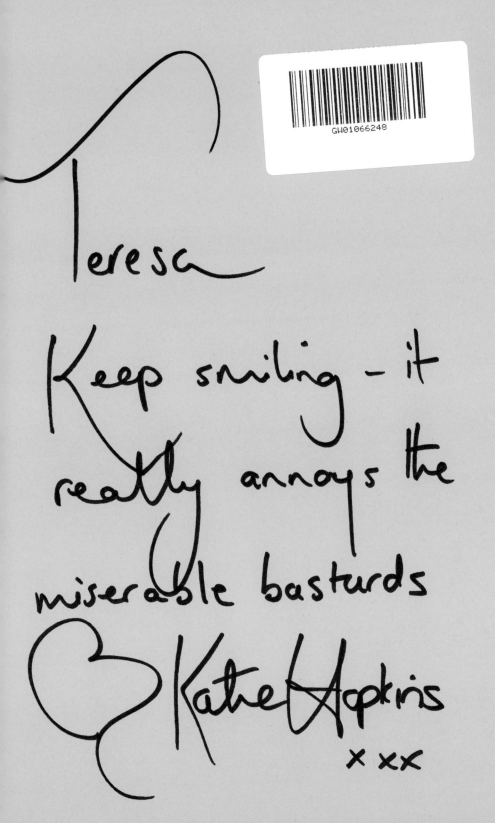

Teresa

Keep smiling – it really annoys the miserable basturds

Katie Hopkins

x xx

KATIE HOPKINS
TRUE

Published by
KHP Ltd

TRUE first published in 2024 by KHP Ltd
21d Chudleigh Road, Exeter EX2 8LB   United Kingdom

ISBN 978-1-7397612-2-6

Set in Minion Pro

Cover design © KHP Ltd 2022
Cover photograph © Katie Hopkins 2024

TRUE by Katie Hopkins

A laugh-out-loud diary from this woman we love to hate, TRUE is Katie at her most entertaining as she shares her struggles just trying to make it through another year.

On these pages, filled with wit and wisdom, you'll hear Katie's voice as she unashamedly overshares and spills all her secrets.

Woven from stories in the news and from the road and her personal life, TRUE reflects us all when we are at our most unpretentious, ordinary and vulnerable – when we are most true to ourselves.

Whether she's describing her 'lazy scissors' sex life, the size of her Christmas turkey or the relentless frustration of booking a venue for her stand-up gigs, nothing is too private, too big or too small to be shared. Trivial, hilarious or harrowing, it's all TRUE.

CONTENTS

INTRODUCTION

I wonder about TRUE as a book. If some PR maniac were to ask, 'What's it about?' I would genuinely struggle to answer.

But for those who know me, even just a little, I think you'll get it.

You'll get that I have no filter, no secrets and nothing to hide.

And you'll get that having spent so many years of my life revealing nothing of my private self, in order to protect it, that it's very liberating to share all of it here now with my very favourite people.

You will know I consider myself to be fundamentally flawed, much more so than most. But that I am unspeakably grateful to still be around on this mad planet, long after I thought the game was up.

And perhaps most importantly, in a world where people seem so desperate to show themselves as marvellous, or happy, or well-dressed, or 'having so much fun with their husband', a year of real life is actually quite a refreshing thing.

My working title for this book was SMALL and you will soon understand why: because it describes all the small things of my ordinary life behind my front door. Just as you have your own secret, private life at home.

I don't have any pearls of wisdom to share and I haven't earned the right to proffer rules for life to anyone. (Nor has Jordan Peterson, actually, but let's not start bitching about weird skinny men this early in the book.)

But I do see that there is real beauty in the small stuff, and big feelings too — tears, laughter, jealousy, lust and the rest.

And that's really the point of this book. Finding the fun in the small stuff of an ordinary woman's year.

Each chapter is a month of my life. In case you're the kind of person that likes to skim-read the summary rather than read the whole damn thing, here are the 12 key lessons from these 12 months:

- **January:** Smart parenting is the avoidance of your own children
- **February:** Shaving your balls does make your member look bigger
- **March:** DTF?
- **April:** Maggoty arses and graffitied vaginas
- **May:** Lovely Mark and Big Boobies in the wine aisle
- **June:** Which comes first, the twat or the money?
- **July:** Black sunshine and weather girls like wildebeests
- **August:** The ten MOST WANTED

- **September:** Young, attractive men do not like to be asked if they are deaf
- **October:** Grinding one out on the beach
- **November:** Dad's DNR
- **December:** Keeping the peace and having a good day

Let's begin…

JANUARY

1 January

'I am giving up boys and men.'

So says my 17-year-old, Poppy, as she sits beside me driving us out to her new caravan accommodation, which goes along with her new farm job.

Ever the independent one, she has passed her test before her older sister, bought and insured her own car, and just wangled herself a new job on a farm and will therefore be moving out before we make it to February.

I ask whether she means both, and in what order. I mean, if you are going to give up one or the other, I would definitely give up boys before men. At least with the latter she might learn something and be taken out for dinner or treated with some kind of respect.

17-year-old boys seem about as useful as a Primark bag in the rain. And equally weak.

'Both,' she declares. And quotes Instagram like it's War and Peace: 'The thing is, if someone isn't adding to my life, or bringing something to my life, why would I be giving away any of my time to them? Surely it's better that I focus on me.'

It turns out there is wisdom to be found in the endless zombie-scrolling after all, and I fully expect this New Year's Resolution to last at least a week – or until the next random male makes a pass at her.

By telling yourself you are off boys and men right up until the point that one comes along who you might actually like, you can mostly avoid the sad truth that you are somewhat lonely and a nice guy would actually be a great thing to have in your world.

She blasts along the country lanes making me wish all at once that she had not bought a more powerful car than mine, and that my death would be immediate and painless.

'I've had four or five offers already,' she says. 'One asked if I could make an exception for him but I told him no.'

Christ on a bike. The New Year is barely at lunchtime and she has already had more relationship offers than I have had cups of coffee. Who are all these boys and men? And how are they making approaches to my daughter?

I wise up to the fact the child has probably announced her New Year's resolution on some kind of social media, given children cannot do anything these days without at least telling anyone who will listen. And in response boys have made offers. It's an old advertising trick and turns out it still works well.

We burn along at an unnecessary speed towards her

new caravan accommodation, the sat nav busily blabbering away, the rancid music of East London blasting out of the radio and some young idiot DJ talking about how he is able to take a pee and be back in his chair inside of three minutes.

That's what passes for talent these days: the ability to not piss yourself and do your job. Standards have fallen.

I have been brought out to this caravan that will be my child's home nominally in order to give it a good clean, but mostly because I have a tendency to over-insert myself into my children's lives and demand to be a part of them.

I recognise I am not really doing this for Poppy. Truth be told, I am here to make myself feel better. As much as I have been encouraging Poppy to leave home since she was able to walk, now that she actually is going to move out I feel very sad that one of my chicks has begun to fledge, and am in desperate need of reassurance that she will be safe and warm and happy away from me.

And standing in the sunshine, overlooking fields and brilliantly white and loved cattle, I see that my middle child will be very happy here. And maybe even prefer it to her life at home. I start to feel better.

Being a mum is a very intricate balancing act between caring, pretending to care, and self-preservation. Even if that simple act of self-preservation is pretending to care. I am suspicious that other mothers do not have these dark thoughts and base their entire lives on kindness and good deeds motivated by nothing more than pure maternal instinct. But I hope I am wrong.

In any case, I never wanted to be associated with the kind of mothers who taught their babies baby sign language or made fruit kebabs. That's some next-level shit right there. If you are teaching your baby to sign before it can speak, you are as-yet unaware that for the next twenty-plus years of your life all that little shit is going to do is ask you for stuff. Or point out horrid truths about you, like you didn't look in the mirror when applying your blusher.

Poppy and I are going through what I would describe as a good phase. Other mothers of teenagers will recognise this parenting term. It's not so much a question of whether the good phase will be followed by a bad one, but when. And these other mothers will agree that our definition of good has morphed a bit since the times we used to spend all day at the beach and call it good. Or eat a meal cooked by someone else, cleared up by someone else, and merely call it good.

A good phase in the teen parenting handbook means they are not killing themselves with drink or drugs, are speaking to you or able to spend two minutes in a room with you without calling you a twat, or are not confined to their bedroom 24/7 avoiding everyone else in the house. If none of these things is happening, you are in a good phase.

Poppy has not only secured a new job and passed her driving test. She is both speaking to me and actually confiding some of her life concerns. Like whether McDonald's will continue to make Chicken Slenders and whether the black box installed to reduce the cost of her car insurance is cramping her life.

My definition of mothering success is survival. One of my brood has already made it to her 18th birthday. I commandeered her 18th birthday lunch to celebrate my excellent parenting skills in keeping her alive this long. The waitresses seemed surprised by my behaviour, alerting me to my extreme narcissism for making this day all about me. But I consider it remarkable that not only did I give birth to a baby I didn't plan and was told to abort at eight months (due to a genetic abnormality), but I sustained the thing all the way to 18.

My youngest, Max, is 14, so within four years I will have kept three very different children alive to the age of adulthood – which means I deserve a bloody medal. The fact I have also managed to stay married for much of this time is part of the circus act called my life.

3 January

Mother has just sent me a WhatsApp of her meat.

She bought it at Morrisons and is very proud of how good it looks in its vacuum packaging sporting a yellow sticker to indicate just what a bargain it was.

Meat has a unique currency in our house. Ever since we were little, meat has had a special value, prized by my culture like virginity in Turkish teens or maleness in the offspring of the Chinese. It may have something to do with Mother's farming heritage, when good meat was an indicator of a good farmer and therefore good breeding, and that is surely what my mother has been desperate to prove throughout my life.

'Just eat your meat' was the last resort of my parents when I was refusing to eat my dinner, which usually consisted of something nightmarish like steak and kidney pie. The last thing I wanted to do on God's green earth was go anywhere near the weird spongy fabric of an organ last used by an animal to rid its own piss of bad stuff.

If you are reduced to eating the organ an animal has used to purify its piss – and that animal was drinking other animals' piss to start with – your tastebuds should be shot off your face.

Nevertheless, other foodstuffs might sometimes be wasted (a crime in Hopkins homes) but meat? Never.

To my mother and father, meat is the centrepiece of any celebration and a symbol of affluent success. Most oldies of their age heralded their progress up the social classes by sending the first 'Arnott' to university. Hopkins success was measured by how plentiful the supply of meat was, and how good the meat was judged to be.

Hence at Christmas we never enjoyed a turkey, but rather an entire pterodactyl. Any farmer could spot my mother and father coming a mile off and would sell them whichever bird was the biggest, baddest, ugliest bastard on their books. Even if it was a frigging ostrich.

I remember Dad going out to the garage to find his hacksaw one year because the bloody bird wouldn't even begin to fit inside the oven and the corpse needed to be dismembered before anyone could try and cook it. Plus, Dad had to get up at 5am to start the cooking process because at 30 minutes per 500g, that was the only way we were going to have roast meat before Boxing Day (a beautiful British name for 26 December).

The lunacy of all this still passes my mother and father by. They still roar 'Meat!' at Christmas and randomly proffer 'MORE MEAT!' at their sons-in-law at spaced intervals, like kings at the feasting tables of old.

Sending me a picture of her discounted meat is not only Mum's way of showing contentment. It's also the promise of a good dinner to come for me and my lot as long as we go around to see her when she says.

It is a form of bribery, I guess, luring us into visiting with the promise of meat, just as a dodgy bar in Benidorm might entice hotties into their premises via free shots. But when you have five adult-sized people living under your roof, free food is not to be sniffed at.

In an ultimate act of rebellion that caused my father to wonder about the meaning of life and the value of family, the other grandchild – the one belonging to my sister – is a vegan. Turns out her vegan-ness was catching because now her whole family are vegans as well. My sister, brother-in-law and niece don't so much as sniff a piece of bacon or cook a chip in lard. My father has still not got over this affront to his meaty generosity and routinely eyes their nut roast with the suspicion he usually reserves for lesbians and black people.

It's not that he is homophobic. Or racist. It's that he is 76 and from the countryside, and new-fangled city notions take a long time to percolate in his parts.

5 January

JustPark would like to know about my parking experience in London. They would like me to leave a review.

I am partly angry at myself for being so easy to access that a parking app has been able to send me an email, and partly angry because I have taken the time to actually read the damn thing.

Even more insulting than my own over-availability, is that a parking app thinks I want to write them a review – for them to use to flog their services – about a bloody car-parking space. I appreciate my life might not be all bikini holiday snaps from Mauritius, or 24/7 on-demand drama. But credit me with at least having more interesting things to do with my life than engage in musings about how I found my parking space. Or how I felt about the communications involved in me finding it.

It's the same with EVRI – right? It just so happens we have the best EVRI delivery driver in the whole of the UK (and this is quite a low bar, believe me) and we all love him. He is super enthusiastic, is the smiliest man you are likely to see in your day, and is especially charming when things go wrong.

But even so, it's anyone's guess quite why EVRI feel the need to let me know my parcel is out on the van, then due to be delivered, then delivered – and then to solicit my feedback on how I feel the delivery went.

It's not as if EVRI are delivering transplant organs, is it? Or life-saving blood supplies after a mass casualty event inside our house? It's not like these items being delivered are special or so precious that I might truly care how they arrive. An extension cable and the odd pack of firelighters are not something I get over-excited about, and frankly if they fell off the back of the lorry and were never delivered at all I would be none the wiser. Until, I guess, I was trying to plug something in or engage in my regular fetish for lighting fires.

Lovely Mark is currently wrestling with the Christmas tree upstairs at the window. It is a great big bloody thing – all seven foot and bushy. However, as fun as it is to put up and as lovely as it looks twinkling away at the window for anyone passing by to see, when Christmas is over and it has to be wrestled downstairs and binned, my job is done. That task sits very firmly in the camp of Lovely Mark.

He is a man of patience, detail and care. As I type these words, he is quietly snipping away at the tree in order to turn it into four-inch pieces that will fit neatly into large plastic sacks. Sometimes I think he has saintly qualities. Other times I wonder if he is just a bit of a moron and speculate that tedious little tasks like this are perfectly suited to his tiny mind. But maybe that's harsh.

Truth is, he likes order and things being done efficiently. To him, snipping a seven-foot tree into four-inch sections to be disposed of is efficient. To me, efficient would be to wrestle the bloody thing from its moorings, haul and shove it down the stairs whole (no doubt injuring myself, the paintwork and the woodwork) and launch it out onto the driveway where I could resolutely ignore it until Lovely Mark saw good sense and tidied it away.

I am all action and no underpants. Lovely Mark is belt and braces and spare pants just in case.

It's a wonder that we are together but somehow our complete lack of compatibility in any regard makes it work.

Yesterday Lovely Mark asked me to get the baubles off the branches to make his onerous task of tree surgery today less challenging. Bored within two minutes, I made a giant pile of baubles on our bed for Lovely Mark to come home to. Which he laughed at, before helping me pack them away properly.

If this book were written by Lovely Mark, he would undoubtedly refer to me as an enormously irresponsible child incapable of doing anything properly or completing any task. And he wouldn't be wrong.

Then again, I'm not the bloody lunatic upstairs trimming a tree into splinters, so I guess that makes me the winner.

6 January

Teenagers are essentially less-useful adults, in the sense that they are about the size of an adult (although they eat more than two adults) but have much less practical functionality in a home setting.

I regard them in the same way I view our two Labradors. They eat, sleep, shit and occasionally look for attention, but in comparison to their size cause a massively disproportionate amount of filth in my nice clean house.

Unlike the dogs, the children also have the power to

be emotionally manipulative and the need for irritating things like lifts and Wi-Fi. They are also relentlessly ungrateful. Dogs have the ability to show gratitude and compassion and are endlessly thrilled by your presence. I cannot say the same of my children, who regard me with suspicion, quite enjoy it when I am taking a nap, and have dismissed many of my best efforts over the years as 'basic parenting'.

How does one answer this unaskable question: given what you know now, if you had your time again, would you have kids?

The easy answer, and the right one, is yes of course. Partly because it's true, partly because it's a question that defies reality, and partly because we all fear the devil will come and bite us on the ass if we acknowledge that there are times we lean out of our bedroom window and silently scream FUCK OFF at our own offspring.

Because of this innate sense of guilt and fear of disapproval, no one talks about how sometimes people feel their kids have ruined their lives. Or at least how they would be much happier if their kids would p*ss off indefinitely. I know one lady who absolutely thinks this way, and I entirely support her in her thinking.

Her daughter recently called her headmaster a c*nt to his face.

I look at this beautiful, lively lady who is having to cope with a monster in her midst, and am completely sympathetic when she says, without hesitation, that she would never have had a daughter if she knew back then what she knows now.

The funniest thing of all is that kids would be outraged if they heard this being said about them. They would be in disbelief. Many would even consider leaving home (if they had somewhere else to go) or reporting their parents to some kind of action line for abused children.

Children believe they are entitled to treat you like dirt and that this is okay, and that you will, naturally, continue to love them unconditionally.

I happen to think unconditional love might be an outdated concept. I do, in fact, love my children unconditionally but that doesn't mean there aren't times when I wonder whether my life would have been better without them.

In the case of my lovely friend, her unconditional love has run out, like a glass that has been drunk from too often. She is now empty of love, unconditional or any other kind, and simply wishes her kid would bugger off and not come back. This is the aspect of parenting no one tells you about. Which is probably just as well.

Poppy is in need of a washing machine at her caravan on the farm. The last farmhand took her washing machine with her, which is a pain in the arse. And my bright idea of renting one at £23 a week has been slightly blown out of the water by the fact NO ONE rents washing machines in the countryside.

I get it. I mean, if you are going to rent washing machines you don't really want to be schlepping them out and about across the landscape. You want to be hitting up tightly-packed terraces in Birmingham. (Do people in Birmingham wash their clothes? I am sure they must.)

However, Poppy needs to be able to wash her farm kit so with my frugal renting plans blown apart, we sit down to order a machine from John Lewis. Not because we are posh, but because Lovely Mark gets staff discount there so it works out way cheaper than anywhere else.

I'm surprised by the gadgets that pop up when Poppy starts the online search. A quick double-check reveals that she has, in fact, been searching for 'wanking machines'.

Given Poppy is knackered nearly 100% of the time, I'd argue that a wanking machine is the last thing she needs. It's also an item rarely sought in the online search bar of John Lewis although, arguably, many of its customers would be much nicer and more smiley people with a little more sex in their life.

We find the cheapest machine and in our shared lack of enthusiasm for this kind of purchase pretend to do sensible things like look at the product specifications and what other customers have said about it.

'I bought this for my daughter and have not had any complaints,' wrote one woman.

I instantly want to meet her and give her a big hug. She knows the torture of living with teenagers. She has clearly seen at least one of her twenty-year-olds leave her home and has done the super-kind thing of buying them a washing machine, and yet the very most she can hope for in return is 'no complaints'.

Kids and gratitude do not go hand in hand. And our

spawn wear their entitlement like no other generation before.

This lovely lady not only raised her kid to adulthood, packed her off to whatever new life she was starting and bought her a new washing machine – she even took the time to go online and write a review for the product despite the dusty husk of emotions that were left from the experience – namely that she received no thanks at all.

I imagine her sitting alone with her cat, wondering what happened to her life.

Poppy tells me to get over myself and books a delivery slot and I realise that I will be out of the country when the blasted thing is set to arrive.

Smart parenting can be the avoidance of your own children.

I smile happily to myself at the thought of her stinking farm kit not ending up in my utility room and my machine, but in hers instead. And grimace slightly at the thought of the phone call I am going to get when it has stopped working after about 2.4 seconds of being rammed full with straw and shite that she hasn't taken the time to wash off first.

9 January

My neighbours appear to be running some kind of feud with me, though this is no surprise because they are as obnoxious as they come and I am not certain there is anyone in the road they actually get along with.

Not that getting along is a benchmark for life. I am

not much into hyper-friendly, pop-round-for-coffee relationships, and much prefer the smile-and-wave-politely-as-we-pass kind of thing. But it is so easy to get sucked in.

These neighbours like to lynch me from time to time. Last time it was because of Poppy's new boyfriend, who drives one of those idiot cars with an extra whatever stuck on it so it makes more noise than it should. Combine this with obnoxiously high-volume music, speeds that should only be seen on a track and a fondness for late hours, and my daughter's choices and behaviour were getting the neighbours' neck hairs up.

They collared me on two separate occasions to warn me of the impending peril she was in (like I wasn't aware of it already).

One of them, brave soul, even came to my car door as I arrived home, to tell my daughter what he thought of her behaviour right in front of me, which I kind of admired and kind of begrudged given this was a) my driveway, b) my daughter and c) I had just got home.

These irritating neighbours, who annoy everyone in the street, have been around to ours numerous other times to issue such bollockings. Once it was for burning leaves and creating smoke. The wife said she was asthmatic and struggling to breathe and told us to put the fire out.

We said no.

My theory is that if she had the breath to get her arse around to our drive and give us a good shouting at, she probably wasn't at death's door, as she claimed. If she was struggling to breathe, she'd need to be conserving energy, not expending it, right?

Another time the husband sent a text to tell us our puppies had ONCE AGAIN marauded their way onto their lawn, were harassing their chickens, and had curled out a large turd on their manicured turf. Mark went round to pick it up.

I admire the puppies in so many ways. When your life is just one big funzy-party and the people who live next door have caged feathery things that run about whenever you rock up, then why not take a massive shit on their lawn just to mark the occasion? I am kind of envious of their free spirit and would love to do the same.

Right now we have a planning application in for an office in the garden and, true to form, the neighbours have complained about it, citing about ten reasons why an office in our garden would be an affront to their home and hearth.

One of their points is that our house is already big enough, so why would we have the need to build another room in the garden? The cheek!

Another concern relates to their MASSIVE hedge, which they say might be damaged in the building process. They make it sound like it's oak trees from the time of Henry VIII when, in fact, it's laurel, which is second only to Japanese knotweed in its ability to grow two metres a day and be almost impossible to kill off.

It's the crippling smallness of it all that gets me, the tiny-ness of these people's lives and thoughts. It must be the hideous emptiness of their own lot that gives them the time and energy to be so petty about other people's business – even those who live right next door.

It makes my flesh feel all weird to even think about, as if I have to physically reject their small-mindedness in case it sticks to any part of me. I want no part of it – I never ever want to be like that. I never want to be peeking from a window watching someone else's life just so I can go and bitch about it to them and issue complaints.

I'd rather have AIDS. At least that suggests I once had a life.

12 January

How much do you reckon what you do in your life and the way you live it affects your kids?

I don't mean the obvious stuff like drink or drugs. I would suggest that if you are off your tits on a Class A drug on a daily basis, the outcome for your kids isn't going to be tremendous. The same applies if you are smashed off your face by 9am and don't even have the mental energy to be outraged by the smugness of the duo that once was Holly and Phil from ITV's This Morning.

I'm talking about the smaller stuff. Like the essence of who you are and what you are about.

I ask this because my girls have just gone quite mad and I think I am the cause. I am uncertain whether to be pleased with myself or slightly afraid.

As some of you know, I consider myself a creature of the road. I am probably at my most comfortable when I am deeply uncomfortable or, at least, in situations others would find intolerably stressful or physically difficult.

I am very happy to step out of my home with a tiny bag, hop on a plane to wherever and not have a single additional bit of logistics planned or in place. As long as I know the thrust of my adventure, or where I have to be on what date, I am not in the slightest bit bothered by how I am going to get there or where I am going to sleep.

It might be a hangover from my army days, it might be personal experience of the road, and it is probably a bit about being able to walk without fear. My 'what's the worst that can happen' answer is 'living to old age'. Nothing terrifies me more than the thought of being less physical in my life or living too long. I notice I am well past my official cut-off point, which was initially 38. Now I am staring 50 in the face.

Even as I sit here in Nashville ahead of a big performance at a great event, I am on the road once more, throwing myself into the sweaty stand-up circuit to practise my craft in front of strangers.

But this time a strange thing has gone on at home in my absence. Poppy, aged 17, has a week off between her last job and her new one. I should add that she will be dropping out of college at this point to work instead, a plan that I applaud.

In her week off she has just booked a trip to Malaga, Spain for five days. On her own. Did I mention she is 17?

There are a few things here.

Firstly, this middle daughter of mine is almost a

cookie-cutter copy of me and how my brain works. If there is a week of emptiness it must be filled. And it shouldn't be filled by anything normal or regular. Imagine the places you can be, imagine where you could go! And just like that you find yourself on a plane to somewhere before you have really worked out what the hell you are going to do there.

I love that she just took off. I know the feeling she will have at some point when she looks about and goes, 'Crap bags, now I am in Malaga on my own.' But I also know the smug satisfaction of doing something for yourself by yourself and surprising lots of people in the process.

Much better this than sitting at home still needing your mother to give you a lift into town and £20 for lunch and a coffee, which seems to be standard practice for lots of teens of wealthier parents out there.

I am also in little position to say anything about any of the choices my kids make, as long as they are exciting, adventurous or expanding how much of life they get to see.

At 17 I was utterly done with the smallness of regular life. One year at college doing A-levels and I was bored out of my tree with the tininess of it all. Even though I still wasn't mad-keen on going to the canteen because it was massive and rammed with people and you needed to find a crowd to sit with. And even though I was certainly not one of the gang that hung out in the snack bar and planned surf trips with excellent hair and wonderfully cool outfits.

But I was still over it, bored of it, itching to be

somewhere else doing something different. So I applied and was selected to go study in Australia for a year.

And that was me – sat on a plane to Australia at 17, ready to live with four families I had never met before and start a new school filled with people I didn't know, on the other side of the planet.

It sounded like a plan that would scare most people. It certainly scared me if I thought about it. So I went right ahead and did it anyway. I was supposed to be 'improving Anglo-Australian relations', and I like to believe that I fulfilled that brief rather well, at least in my personal life.

In a political sense, possibly not quite so much.

I would return to Australia a number of times over the coming years – notably in 2021, when I would be accused of 'flouting Covid regulations' for threatening to run naked down a corridor, have my visa cancelled and get deported and banned from the entire continent for three years.

As the French like to say, I don't regret a thing.

FEBRUARY

Where the hell did February go?

I mean, I recognise it is only 28 days instead of the standard 30 or 31, but even so. Having been around on this weird little planet for 48 years, the difference of two or three days doesn't really factor in, now does it?

I now see that a month really can seem to 'fly by', as old people like to say. Which is why I find myself quoting my fellow dog walkers in the park when they have nothing in particular to say: where did February go?

In truth, many of the days of February are bloody long indeed. January may officially be the shittiest month of the year, but by the time it gets to February and it is still grey and dark much of the time, I am officially over winter.

I made a pact with my family that I will never do another winter in the UK, at least not full-time. I have even made a point of repeating this to each of them individually whenever I felt they looked as if they might be receptive to this kind of Big News from their mother.

None of them feels this is particularly big news at all.

Lovely Mark took the news as if it were something he had been anticipating all along: 'Okay love, where would you like to spend it?' was his reply. Which is classic Marky Mark.

Most people (including myself) would instantly be thinking: okay, but what does YOUR decision mean for ME? As in: wait, if Mark is not going to be here for the whole winter, what will that mean for ME? Who is going to do all the dog walks / washing up / sorting the fire / taking ME out for lunch / cuddling up under the duvet / and other less fun chores, like unblocking toilets?

But not lovely Mark. I think sometimes he sees himself as a kind of facilitator of my happiness. Whenever I have an utterly mad idea his first response is to wonder how I would like to make that happen, instead of muttering, 'Silly cow!' and vowing to divorce me at the first opportunity, as I am pretty sure most sane men, ground down by 15 years of marriage, would want to say to me.

Somehow he still sees life with me as an adventure and is still happy to be part of it.

The answer to where I would like to go is actually Mexico – Puerto Morelos, to be precise, officially my favourite place in the world to date. Partly because it represents an escape from everything associated with Western Europe, partly because it is where I spent three weeks waiting to break into the US, and partly because it is where I wrote Help!, my last book. Cast away in my little bit of paradise, writing away while waiting to break into the States at a time when Brits weren't allowed entry, was so desperately romantic it is burned into my soul.

Mark suggests Spain. It's his version of a practical compromise: much warmer, with the definite possibility of sunshine, but also close enough for me to pop over for four days and be back again at the weekend.

But as we know, practical and compromise are not really part of my specialist skill set. Bonkers and disastrous are much more me, don't you think? And these two excellent traits result in much of the fun we share in these pages and in other parts of my dramatic life.

Either way, the commitment has been made. I will not spend another winter in the UK. Seven months of unrelenting greyness is more than any menopausal woman should have to withstand and given I have always looked at 50 years as my aspirational life expectancy, I only have another two winters left and cannot afford to be buggering about waiting for a glimpse of sun in the one blue-sky day we might get before April.

'It's so lovely in the sun!' my mother will affirm on that one day we actually get to see the sky. Or another of her optimistic classics: 'It's lovely as long as you're out of the wind.'

It's this kind of British stoicism that results in so many of us enduring our utter bullshit weather for so long.

It's lovely once you are out of the wind. Well yes, I am sure it is. It would also be lovely in the scorching heat of the sun dressed only in half a thong, but we don't have that, do we?

Being 'out of the wind' involves tremendous effort,

or bus shelters that smell of piss. It certainly involves cowering behind a wall or similar, which is not usually how I like to enjoy my outings.

It is so much easier to be in the full sun. So much easier to be in the warm sea, so much easier to not have three hundred coats on plus an entire duvet sewn to your back before you even attempt to face the day.

For those who don't live here, trying to function as a human is really bloody difficult in this country. If you do muster up the enthusiasm to actually leave your house or go out (God forbid), when you either arrive at your destination or return home, you have to undress. This is the equivalent of unwrapping a mummy. You end up with a mountainous pile of hats, gloves, coats, sweaters, etc – just to have a pint. People say the two things you can be certain about in life are death and taxes. In fact, there is a third thing: if you attempt to visit a pub in winter, you will leave one glove behind, and it will never be seen again.

Odd gloves and odd socks. These are the things that punctuate the seven months of festering greyness that call themselves autumn, winter and early spring here in the UK.

10 February

Lovely Mark has had something of a makeover. Much of it against his will, and certainly against his better judgement.

If he had his way, he would be walking around looking like a cross between a very sick AIDS patient and a victim of extreme Nazi cruelty in a concentration camp. He believes the answer to thinning hair is to shave it all off so that the bits that are thin aren't peeping out between the bits that are not.

This is all very well if you are slightly chubby or have a face that says glee. Somehow, missing hair on jolly people is totally fine, if not endearing.

Mark has neither of these faces. Due to his aversion to fatty foods, cakes, crisps, chocolate or any of the normal things that help us get through life, Mark's face is more angled than a protractor. He has none of my puffy features or sagging skin, and for many years easily looked a third of his actual age.

Now he has hit sixty, left unattended he just looks sick. With a fully shaved head I would bet he was half-way through chemo.

So my big effort has been to soften this all up so as to have a cuddlier version of my husband and so that he won't scare the kids where he works.

Longer hair has very much helped. Mark strongly objects to older men who try and cling on to their hair, but I have patiently explained this is not what he is doing. What he is doing is sharing the hair he has left with the community.

My next effort was to snazzy him up a bit and by chance (must be a God thing), I stumbled on a picture of Robbie Williams looking particularly hot and yet age-appropriate and decided this was the look I now needed to persuade Lovely Mark would be a good idea … if not actually his all along. Us girls know how this system works: we have a good idea, we persuade our husband it was his idea, and because he knows all his ideas are good ideas, he does it.

As luck would have it, this time of the year is my birthday and also our anniversary – yes, we got married on my birthday so I couldn't bloody well forget – and it was time for our annual pilgrimage to anywhere to escape life for two nights together.

This window of calm and affection allowed me to push forward with my Robbie Williams plan for Mark's head.

The Turkish barber looked less convinced.

I am always wary of Turkish barber shops. I think they are eminently cool places and love the fact that men with WAY too much hair everywhere (specifically on their backs) always frequent these places to have it shaved off, or out, or up. Nose hair, ear hair, eyebrow hair, back hair… and God-knows-where-else hair.

I mean, it's basically sheep shearing for young men with dark hair.

These barbers are pretty smart dudes when you think about it, meeting endless demand with cheap supply – namely a razor, a flame and some hookah pipes. Or in extreme cases some kind of scythe to get through the worst of it.

I digress. I am not wary of Turkish barbers because of the amount of hair they chop through, but because my relationship with places like Turkey has not always been the most cordial. I think President Erdogan is something close to the devil walking, and I've never been entirely supportive of the Muslim takeover of our fine country.

But Lovely Mark is not going to become Robbie Williams by turning to the local gentleman hairdresser in our tiny town, now is he?

So in I went. I agreed with Lovely Mark that I would say my bit and then leave, so that:

a   I would not look like some kind of weird mother with a child-husband

b   I would avoid becoming any kind of attention trap. My biggest nightmare would be that the men or their mates would know my name and want to take selfies; this was not part of the romantic escape plans.

Anyway, I showed the barber the Robbie picture in question and he looked a bit scared for Mark and for this decision. He asked me if I was sure, which seemed odd because it is actually Mark's head we were discussing. But I fully respect the fact he didn't look at Robbie, then look at the remaining hair on Lovely Mark's head and laugh.

Quite the opposite. And so he set about the transformation and I snuck out of there while I was ahead. The barber even promised to wait for my return before he took a flaming torch to Mark's ears – which is what I call customer service.

Returning ten minutes later expecting to find Robbie Williams singing 'Angels' to me – naked – I was a bit disappointed, but I covered it by giggling nervously.

Lovely Mark now has something resembling a balding mullet – which I absolutely love. It has attitude. It says, 'I am not giving up.' I'd argue it also says, 'I am still having sex,' which is important for a man at his time of life.

And on that note, Mark really got on board with the whole hair-removal plan following the flaming torch applied to his ear holes. I have been suggesting for quite a while now that his man-garden could do with some attention. I see the hypocrisy in this, given that on most days you could grate cheese with my leg hair. But Lovely Mark scuttled off with his shaver on Sunday and came back looking jolly pleased with himself. I think the man-sculpting of the genital area has been achieved.

I keep meaning to have a fumble in the jungle and check it out, but for the last three nights have fallen asleep as my head touched the pillow, so I am none the wiser. One Sunday morning when I am feeling perky, I promise to get a grip and let you know.

13 February

As promised, I am back with the update and it is good news. Lovely Mark has indeed sculpted his man-zone and the reason I married him now stands proud, like a nuclear warhead looking vaguely menacing, which is excellent. Before, it was all a bit early 70s Apollo with the clouds of furry hair threatening to engulf the magnificence of the main event.

Married sex is hilarious when you think about it. If you stick together in the way that marriage was originally intended, you end up having sex with the same person for (let's say) 30 years.

I say 'the same person' but who can honestly say they have been the same person for all those years? We are the same in our hearts, we may have the same personality traits or things that make us happy. But physically and sexually we are anything but.

You will have felt attractive, and as ugly as a chimp with a chaffed arse. You will have felt overwhelmed with the need to hump like a rabbit needing another brood, and also wanted nothing more than to be in bed on your own with a book and not have to even touch feet.

You will have been fatter or thinner or happier or less so or any and everything in between. You may have been overwhelmed with attraction for your husband and revolted at the thought of going anywhere near him. And vice versa. And that's before you start adding in the stuff that really screws up your sex life or attraction to your other half – like kids or cutting toenails.

I understand that kids and cutting toenails do not appear to be on a linear scale of importance, but both can have quite a massive effect on one's sex life.

Many good women I know much prefer to sleep alone and some have even been bold enough to agree this sleeping set-up with their husband. They have separate bedrooms and visit each other when the mood takes.

Lovely Mark and I have been through all the stages there are. We were once so desperate to be having sex all the time that we had it in a field, and made early morning booty calls before work even began just so we could make it through the day.

Imagine that now! Imagine setting your alarm for 5am and getting up before you needed, just to have a shower and shave and moisturise so that when your future husband visited, your hotness was set to FIRE… You could not pay me to make that kind of effort these days. I love Lovely Mark with all my heart, but imagine making yourself all fancy just to perform like an acrobat at the Cirque de Soleil between the sheets at 5.30am. And then go on to do a full day's work!

Sometimes I think I may have taken the whole sales pitch for being the next Mrs Cross a bit too far. I reckon I massively over-promised in the affair / dating years and have probably underdelivered for about the next 15. A woman can only do so much.

When I think about dating again or imagine these lovely ladies on dating apps going out of an evening to meet someone they have taken the time and effort to swipe and connect with, I feel exhausted. Imagine the effort! Imagine pretending to be interested in someone when you are not. Or – my biggest fear – meeting someone for a drink and knowing in 2.2 seconds that they are absolutely not for you but having to spend time with them for fear of being rude.

I see young people on dating shows who have zero chemistry between them but are still kind enough to say, 'But it was great to meet them and great to spend a fun evening together!' I am sorry, but that's a bare-arsed lie. Who wants to have dinner with a potential date only to find they have zero sexual interest in them? Eating is a fine idea but if you aren't going to be at it like horny toads at some point, you might as well sit at home and have a sandwich.

The only way round this is the way we used to do it as young ones: test the goods in a club or pub. Only if you were certain you couldn't keep your hands off each other in the darkness did you agree to meet in daylight.

That seems a far more sensible way around the 'dating' problem.

I am happy to say that Lovely Mark and I made it through the mid bit of marriage where you only have enough energy to occasionally give each other a hug, and got back to a new kind of rhythm where you can still have a sex life but without the majority of the effort.

Over-excitable young men on social media call me a MILF. (If you are blissfully unaware, this stands for Mother I would Like to F*ck). Some just boldly type WOULD (meaning they would sleep with me). There is no consideration given as to whether I was offering such favours or would myself be willing to accommodate them.

I think the young machismo idea is that all women are waiting for them to deign that they would, at which utterance we are expected to fall on our backs, legs akimbo, to gratefully receive their offering. This blows my mind.

The latest missive I received, which confused me no end, was, 'DTF?'

I was unsure of what this meant, although the punctuation clearly indicated a question. I was forced to Google it in case it was an acronym for something I needed to know, or ought to know as the mother of teenage girls. It is, indeed, this question: down to f*ck?

It's a funny old world, because boys used to say a girl was 'well up for it' if she seemed a bit over-friendly or they heard from a mate she had banged their brother or whatever. But now up is down, and you need to be down to fuck, as opposed to being up for it.

It is terribly flattering that these young men are asking, or saying that they would. Ditto being called a MILF. I wouldn't want to bust their illusion or detract from the idea that I am super-hot, but I have to say my very favourite kind of sex now is quite different to what any of them might be imagining.

It's called Lazy Scissors and it is epic.

Can I just add at this point, it's not called that in real life. I didn't look this up in a book and you won't find it in the Kama Sutra or 50 Ways to Keep Your Love Life Alive. It's my own name for my very favourite way to have sex with my very own husband.

Can I also add that it has absolutely nothing to do with needlework or sewing, as I cannot stand either? No actual scissors are involved in the performing of this position.

If you are married or have been married for any amount of time, I am sure you will have your own version of Lazy Scissors. I encourage you to think of a name that describes it in a natty way. The greatest thing about Lazy Scissors is that it can be performed without the unnecessary removal of the pyjama top, minimising any bare-skin-meets-cold-air issues. Plus, both of you are still fully under the duvet and both still lying down, so no one feels like they are the one making all the effort.

The other great thing is that at no point are your heads too close together so you can have all the morning breath you want without anyone being put off. And yet, you are still managing to have sex after 20 years of marriage and that has to be a win.

If you have been married for a couple of decades and are still swinging off chandeliers and attaching nipple tassels as you launch yourself on top of your husband, I commend you. You are the aspiration and you set the standard for us mere mortals out here. This is dedication to service and you rock. I also suspect you live somewhere hot and sunny where the fear of getting a cold arse does not hold you back. I see couples who are just like this and they both share a knowing twinkle, like they struck gold but are keeping it a shiny secret.

And if you are 50 and your marriage is just about over and you cannot wait to be back out there being banged harder than a big bass drum at a Gabriel Prokofiev concert, I say go girlie. How brilliant to escape the tedium of what wasn't making you happy, to launch forth and find things that do. And how marvellous to invest energy and effort in making yourself the best you can feel for someone else to appreciate you. To all of you, I say the gloriousness of such a thing is not lost on me, not at all.

I meet many women who are so ready to start a new life on their own and I feel nothing but excitement for them. Many were married to older men who just went on getting older, and most are yearning to feel free again. Or to feel something again – and with that as a starting point they will not be disappointed.

Or perhaps you live alone and are actually very content that way. Perhaps you have no wish to bring complications into your life or to risk your heart again when you are happy as you are. Perhaps your dog or your cat is really the soul that understands you best and you are at peace with that. I see men and women like this who are splendid in their solitude and don't need explaining or company or excuses – they just are, and they're happiest that way.

And I think that's kind of all of us at different times. We are not 'the same person' throughout our lives. We are all the things above: the adventurous, the content, the ready-for-anything and the gymnast-with-a-heavy-interest-in-porn. Or the other half of a lazy scissor. All of us, at one time or another, have been one of those things and I think that is what makes us splendid.

MARCH

3 March

I set out into March slightly beset by worry. It's a big month in my family as far as birthdays go and God forbid I miss one of them and cock things up.

Post brain surgery – and perhaps well before that, but I like to use brain surgery as an excuse because it is dramatic and I am all about the drama. But post brain surgery I have the short-term memory of an elderly patient in a care home.

Actually, the elderly patient has one up on me at this point, as anyone in a care home pretty much has a free pass to behave as disgracefully as they please. They are expected to do loopy stuff like turn up naked for breakfast or go wandering off and be found face down in aisle 6 at Asda.

I don't have that free pass and despite my best efforts to impress upon my mother and sister that I cannot be blamed for any of my forgetful or odd behaviour, somehow I am still expected to get the right card to the right person on the right day.

It's one of the many reasons I have never been asked and should never be asked to be a godparent. I would be absolutely crap at it.

Good godparents do nurturing things like care about someone else's kid and remember to buy them presents at appropriate moments like birthdays and Christmases. I'd have failed at every turn. I think it telling that my old friends – despite being my friends – have always been quite certain I was not the sort of person they would trust their kid with in the event that their own untimely demise left their little darling orphaned. I suspect many of them would choose a care home over the idea of Aunty Katie taking charge.

My sister feels exactly the same way. And yet I am supposed to remember the godforsaken month in which her daughter is turning 18. I know that the penalty for forgetting will be that I won't be spoken to for some considerable time.

Then there is the Mothership herself. She says she doesn't want a present. She says I have given her enough, what with this or that. But actually the Mothership loves a fuss – of any description. So I can't afford to cock up her birthday, either.

And finally, as if all that wasn't enough for my tiny, tired pea brain, it is Mothering Sunday.

As anyone with a mother and kids will know, there is a delicate dance involved in managing this day. You need to make a fuss of your own mum, and the responsibility for this gets worse each year. What if this is the last year you have your mum for Mothering Sunday and you fail to do something nice or special and then have to live with regret? No one wants regret in their life.

But I also have to manage the fact that I really don't want my kids to make a big public fuss of me, but I do definitely want them to care and make a private fuss by way of hand-drawn cards or perhaps even a candle or a lovely-smelling thing.

Ultimately I want everyone to be happy but these days are laced with the kind of invisible hand-grenades that can detonate at any moment, leaving people feeling forgotten or miserable.

I think this is true for many women on 'special days' like Mothering Sunday, who frankly feel SHAT upon at every turn. Women are the backbone of everything, and doing everything is repetitive and thankless and that kind of gets highlighted on 'special' days if you are left not feeling very special at all. Men and kids can often seem utterly ungrateful and as thick as mince. It's just a truth.

Having a day where you are supposed to be made to feel special but aren't, kind of makes things worse, not better.

People like to talk about men being from Mars and women being from Venus but that's just twiddling with words to make men feel better. Women are bloody grafters and men are instinctively selfish to protect their own sperm. That's more the truth of it and the actual book title they should have gone with.

You all know I love men. Specifically manly men. And men that get their hands dirty. And I have been known to do dark deeds with some of them that I probably shouldn't have done.

But the fact is, women are there working a job, bringing up kids, deciding what's for tea, vacuuming carpets, trying to keep the daily tidal wave of filth that flows through the door to a gentle roar, and somehow still pretending to like sex once in a while to relieve their husbands – who are, sometimes, handy to have around. It's a wonder any of us survive past 40.

It doesn't help when you have wunderthumps like Holly Willbooby or whatever her name is, with seven kids and an influencer's budget, wafting around looking fresh and perky holding a perfect bunch of flowers. Or posing with their family, all wearing matching shades of taupe-and-cream cashmere, in perfect lighting to show how they are 'spending Mothering Sunday'. That, my friends, is utter tripe. That is not how they are spending their day. That is part of their day, which they manufacture and curate with the help of assistants, wardrobing and hair and make-up, in order to post to their followers and fans who love it.

And all of that is perfectly fine unless you mistake it for their reality, which it is not. Their reality is a lot of keeping-up appearances for clicks or cash or both, and that is a whole lot less fun than it looks.

10 March

As much as I hope that spring is finally around the corner and this godforsaken, never-ending winter of grey and gloom is over, I am harbouring a concern.

I like to pretend to myself I am not all that vain. As long as I run and am not fat, then I'm trying my best and I would never have surgery, botox or fillers to improve my appearance. However, in truth, there are several things I am self-conscious about, and my varicose vein is one of them.

And this little sucker is not getting any smaller.

In fact, to my alarm, over this past winter it has expanded upwards towards my crotch and can clearly be seen bulging half-way up my thigh, like some particularly gnarly ivy my grandmother would have sawed down in a heartbeat.

'Various veins' my father calls them, laughing away to himself in his chair at the misfortune of others, particularly mine.

My grandmother had them, as did my mother, so now of course, I do too. I fail to see how genetics and heredity make things more acceptable. People suck on their teeth and say, 'Ah yes, your grandmother suffered with those,' as if that makes it better.

I have been around for 48 years, my mother is 74, and her mother was 90-odd when she died. My point is that the medical profession has had at least 100 years – a century! – to come up with a solution to these ugly snake veins and has failed to bother because they aren't sexy and no one wants to talk about ugly legs. And that's just working on the basis that my grandmother was the first person to ever have an ugly vein, which is improbable. I fancy Queen Victoria suffered horribly with them; she just has that kind of face.

If men didn't get to wear trousers and were forced into skirts, I can guarantee the cure for varicose veins would have been discovered way back when, as much a priority as penicillin.

My point is that as spring approaches and the old legs are going to have to come out, the vein is going to become more of an issue than ever. Partly because it now extends the full length of my leg, partly because it throbs like a mofo, and mostly because I should have done something about it over the long winter of darkness.

I want this thing cut out. But is that vanity? Or medical necessity? I suspect it is a bit of both.

I have just tried getting in touch with BUPA, who are frankly about as useful as a penis-flavoured lollipop. After waiting twenty minutes for a digital representative, I have now been typed at to say there will be another 14-minute wait to talk to a customer service person, who I strongly suspect will also be AI.

If I WAS suffering from something with the potential to kill me, the Grim Reaper would easily win over a digital customer service representative from BUPA. I'd be dead before BUPA deigned to actually help.

Which morons take on the role of 'digital customer service representative' anyway? Who wants to work from home and be paid by a company to pretend to answer random queries from people – without ever truly resolving an issue or solving a single problem?

I don't know why these people still get to call themselves support when support is the last thing they offer. Far better to be monikered the Exhaust Team, designed to be as slow and as dull and as politely unhelpful as possible until you are so exhausted by their effort that you give up.

Only the truly desperate will persevere. Which is part of the system. Which is why I am determined this time not to give up.

I will persevere. I will pay to get this thing cut out. And I will put an end to this nonsense.

Every time I get my leg out with its ugly vein, my mother makes the sort of face you make when you get your nipple caught in the door. Or someone puts vinegar on a wound. She visibly flinches, despite the fact she was the one that gave me these festering veins in the first place.

Honestly. The shit we have to put up with as women.

15 March

Quokkas are my new favourite animal. If you don't know what a Quokkas is, you are not alone. Nor did I until about 20 minutes ago when one came up on my Instagram feed but there is something about the Quokkas you need to know. Hang tight.

I am uncertain how Insta knows just exactly what to show you at different times of your life – sometimes it is just damn creepy.

I have never mentioned or spoken about my issues with my spine, but I have a particularly annoying curve in my back (scoliosis), and fractured my T6 vertebra during my army training because of it. Weirdly, Insta seems to know about this injury and sends me content about physiotherapists and other exercise maniacs for exactly this section of spine. It is as if Insta feels my pain and sends me ways to fix it.

How does Insta know about my back? Is it watching me struggle when it aches? Is it spying on me when I am on my exercise-roller thing? I don't even want to think about it.

I know the algorithm can work out the best content for me, and knows how long I spend looking at certain content, but still, it's freaky. As is the fact that I get directed to so much content about women losing their shit. Although I much prefer honest women losing their shit to pretty women showing off clothes. Fuck those bitches.

But this morning something altogether better happened and I was gifted the image of a Quokkas holding its baby Quokkas in its arms.

The Quokkas looks like a cross between a particularly happy beaver and a koala on acid. Something about its face means it looks like it is permanently smiling and having a good time. Plus, it is fairly small and very furry, as most cute things tend to be.

Turns out the Quokkas is a legend in the mothering department, too.

If a fully smiling Quokkas is attacked by a predator, it

will literally prise its fluffy baby Quokkas from its chest and lob it at the predator while it makes a run for it and escapes.

None of this 'throwing yourself in front the bus to save your kids' shit for the Furry One. Oh no! Much better to sacrifice your kid and leg it – you can always make another one and all that.

I admire its honesty, its integrity and its dedication to self-preservation.

After all, as the goody-two-shoes set are always saying, you can't take care of others if you don't take care of yourself. Which seems to answer the Quokkas dilemma perfectly. Not only have you taken care of yourself – you have also fed the 'others' you were supposed to take care of to an angry-looking dingo or python.

And that, my friends, is smart mothering right there.

18 March

Did you know that female dogs go about the place dripping from their vaginas?

I appreciate that question may have come a little out of the blue and if you were just shoving half an M&S tuna sandwich in your gob, you might be gagging a bit. But honestly, I had no idea either.

I knew we were getting girl dogs. (I refuse to call them bitches. No matter what they do and no matter how much cleaning up I have to do after them, I think that term should be reserved for skinny, mean-natured women who permanently waft about in Lululemon gear.)

I just never knew girl dogs had actual periods of their own. And I absolutely never knew that dog owners consider it to be normal to have to go around their house clearing up after dogs who are dripping from their inflated foofs.

I don't know whether I was being thick or ignorant or just a bit naive. Possibly I never needed to think about such things, just as one doesn't need or want to spend too much time thinking about how people with bowel cancer actually die.

But now I know. And frankly it is disgusting.

As I type, my sofa has a towel over it, my lounge carpet is covered in a decorator's sheet, and both animals are confined as often as possible to the kitchen, which has wipe-clean tiles. It's like having an incontinent mother-in-law to stay in her final weeks of life, but without the certain knowledge that the end is nigh.

On investigation I have learned that dog owners can get wise to when their female dog is planning to start dripping blood all over the place by spotting that their dog's foof has 'swelled up'.

And does it ever. I am embarrassed to walk them through the village at this point. This is a place where women keep themselves to themselves and everyone pretends to lead a perfect life behind their perfectly manicured hedges. Here, people do not parade vaginas about willy nilly, whether it's their own or their dogs'.

The aerodynamics of my two Labradors are now ridiculous. The swollen vaginas on these girls are like the rear spoiler of an F1 car, gripping them to the road by their smooth underbellies.

Their lady-parts look like small inflatable boats, all puffy on the sides. I am pretty certain a crafty enough band of Somalis could climb aboard my Labradors and make it across the Channel using only their swollen bits and a paddle.

How the hell is this whole set-up thought to be okay?

You are supposed to avoid male dogs at this point in case they decide to climb aboard your pet pooch and give your drippy dogs a good humping. I know Labradoodles and Cockapoos are all very trendy. But undoubtedly my two lunatics would be humped by some ugly balding pit bull mongrel and we'd end up with twenty-four labrapitbulls. And no one wants one of them.

I have now acquired dog nappies from some poor Chinese person flogging their cheap and nasty products online. I ordered extra large but rather forgot that our Asian friends have a penchant for small dogs that can fit in your pocket. Or tiny things that look like rats on a string.

So the nappies I now have for my dogs are a bit on the tight side – more G-string nappy than the full Pampers experience. But they at least stop the random dripping on my carpets and have the added advantage that I can no longer see their flapping foofs clapping at me sarcastically. Nor do I have to watch them lick their bits, which makes me physically retch.

All of which leads me to wonder whether this phenomenon is happening to all girlie animals all over the planet. No one has ever talked about it on any wildlife documentary I have ever watched. Presumably cows do it? And lionesses? And turtles?

Given monkeys are basically humans (I'd argue more sophisticated than many) perhaps there are times of the month when they simply want to lie under a tree with a hot-water bottle and eat chocolate, and no-one has yet noticed?

I think it best that I return to not thinking about it. And for now put up with the humiliation of having two gun dogs in nappies and my usually stoic disposition put out by being surrounded by a sea of dog periods and flappy foofs.

20 March

I have a stalker – and not a good one.

This particular sh*tbag has been dedicating his life (a small and pointless one, I should add) to trying to get my venues to pull their shows. And very successful he has been, too.

He has a magic formula that works wonders, and in itself evidences the very sad state of a society in which the fear of giving offence and the amplification of the suggested offence is enough to make a venue run a mile from a highly profitable venture that would keep itself and its staff in business for a good month.

I am not certain I can mention this little arsehole's name right now because there is the making of a happy ending to this story. For now we will call him The Rabbit.

The Rabbit dedicated his Facebook page to me, with the title 'Katie Hopkins is a C*NT', and explained that his full-time occupation was to get venues to pull the shows they had agreed to.

The Rabbit appears to be gay, though I am certain he has at the very least considered outing himself as trans, as that is so much more fashionable and would get him extra kudos among the cancel freaks he entertains.

On this Facebook page of his, he brags about his conquests (meaning venues he's pulled, not sexual partners; I doubt he has ever made a legitimate sexual conquest without the aid of Rohypnol). He even bragged of his certainty of being arrested for harassment at some point, such was the intensity of his campaign against the staff at venues selling tickets with my name on.

The basic system is this:

1   Contact venue all wide-eyed and innocent, suggesting that perhaps they did not know who 'this Katie Hopkins character' is and then detail all her most dreadful doings. Said doings need not be factual. They can just be the worst things you could write that would never be tolerated, and you can add details like 'arrested for hate speech' or 'banned for racism'. None of these things are factually accurate, but that does not matter.

2   Make it clear you are someone to be feared because you are gay / trans / lesbian / bi-curious / black / disabled / tick as appropriate.

3   Begin a relentless campaign of phone calls and emails
    to everyone involved with the venue, from management
    to the lady in the ticket booth, particularly the latter.
    And find a point of weakness, or someone who agrees
    with you a bit, or someone who is not a supporter of
    Katie Hopkins because they are fat.

4   Aggressively escalate this campaign against the staff
    member until they feel worried for their safety or are
    scared enough to tell management going ahead with
    the event is a bad idea.

5   Involve other artists performing at the theatre. Try
    and get one of them to say they won't perform if Katie
    Hopkins is performing there. This works best with acts
    that typically can't sell a single ticket but are in any way
    whatsoever related to the above-mentioned tickbox
    selection.

6   Once one other act agrees to pull out, contact the local
    press. Give them the Katie hook, add that other acts
    are pulling out, get one local person to say they are
    'shocked this far-right racist is being given a platform'
    and boom, an easy story for a lazy-arsed content writer
    who knows the story will get clicks because it has the
    name Katie Hopkins in it.

7   Start a petition, get a local lefty councillor to back it,
    add more venom and hate onto any staff member still
    answering the phone to you –
    – and eventually the venue will pull.

It works nearly every time. Even in respected theatres

where I have created a relationship with a member of management who is a supporter. Even when we have SOLD OUT 500 seats and the venue knows it will be their biggest night for six months. Even then, the spineless fools will still pull.

And remember, this is just in the venues that we target to book. We would never even try and book a council-run theatre, 'Bedford Leisure' or any such place. Anywhere with even a sniff of government or local council about it and we give it a wide berth. Not because we couldn't fill these places – we could. But because we know that spineless lot would fold at the merest hint of an issue.

Plus, most are run by some lefty freak who believes what they think should dictate what others are allowed to come and see. It's the most patronising thing in the world. Our 'elders and better' on the left actively believe, with absolute certainty, that the little people need someone to advocate on their behalf. Those who consider themselves intelligent and superior actively believe you should not have the choice to decide who you should pay to see or hear or listen to.

They are your self-appointed guardians, protecting you from the damaging effects of listening to me.

And so it goes on. The Rabbit applies this process to every single venue I book and in 2023 alone 43 venues pulled my shows.

Let me say this very clearly and somewhat for the record: this is not okay.

Every single time it is like a full punch to the gut and

each time I take a good punching from another venue, I know that this little weasel with his lies gains power, and I have to walk forwards knowing I am about to get punched again, each time harder than the last.

I know that these punches will make me sick and ache.

I know I will then have to read about things I have never thought or said and events that have never happened, and see the words 'arrested for hate speech' printed in the press and taken as true.

I have read The Rabbit bragging about how he intimidated people to the point they were terrified.

And I can expect the next venue to pull because the last 40 did.

Some losses are more painful than others. In Stafford I worked so hard to get the venue to hold. My amazing supporters emailed the venue to thank them for taking a stand when The Rabbit came for them. And we had 550 amazing people looking forward to being together and having a lovely night out.

AND STILL THEY PULLED. Worse still, the coward at the venue who knew me didn't even pick up the phone to let me know. The first I heard about it was when ticket holders contacted Lovely Mark asking why their tickets had been refunded.

Email from Keith Harrison, Stafford Gatehouse Theatre:

Tickets still selling steadily and we're confident we'll hit a sell-out before the big day. All looking good.
Best wishes,

Keith Harrison
Marketing Manager,
Stafford Gatehouse Theatre, Freedom Leisure

Truly, for a military woman like myself, that single act of cowardice hurt more than the punches and the lies. The fact that a man I have spent time chatting to and being open with has not found the decency to ring me man to man and own up to his lack of spine, is overwhelming. I don't want to be disappointed in people. I want to find the best in people. But small men like this one make it very challenging at times.

I would like to say quietly to both Keith Harrison and Gary Carter at the Stafford Gatehouse Theatre, please be better in future. If you want to cancel a woman like me, and pull the freedom of choice from 550 people, at least have the testicles to call me in person and allow me to notify my wonderful audience in a manner that befits their investment of time, money and support for your venue.

You may mess with me, you may be willing to throw me under the bus and you may think hiding is easier than treating me with the kindness I deserve from you.

But you do not get to treat my lovely audience that way. My audience deserves better than you throwing their money back in their face. The supporters who took the time to email you to thank you for holding out (for a few weeks) deserve better than you.

Because you receive council funding – which is taxpayer's cash – you were willing to spit on the ordinary people who wanted to come and have a nice night out and laugh and feel better. You'd rather stay out of trouble and keep your little jobs than make a stand for what is right and help persuade your puny bosses to make better choices.

Yet despite all of this – the punches, the sadness and the obvious disappointment – if you would like to make good on the contract we had and the tickets I sold, I will come back to the Gatehouse Theatre Stafford and perform for my lovely family-on-the-road. Because the truth is that I love them more than you can hurt me. And my love for our side is far greater than the injuries I sustain in bringing us together.

Keith and Gary, I invite you to man up. Why not give people the freedom to choose who they come and see?

Want to come and see Katie Hopkins? Buy a ticket. Don't like her? Can't stand her? Stay home.

26 March

Train travel in the UK has become near impossible.

Even at the point of booking you know your scheduled journey is more of an aspiration than a thing likely to happen. There is a timetable, there is a seat reservation but there is absolutely zero certainty of there being either a train or a seat to sit on. Or if there is a train, of it running even vaguely on time. There will certainly be no seat reservation and you will be standing next to a toilet for three hours.

Today is no exception. Despite being the most important day of the year for footballers from Plymouth, trains from Plymouth have 'gone down' due to a 'signalling error', meaning fans will be drunk and pissed off in the wrong city.

For me trying to get to Manchester, it means my train that was 'on time' when I woke up has suddenly became a non-train and is cancelled completely. Passengers like me – I say 'passengers' but there are no passengers if there's no train to get on; you're just a person with nowhere to go and no way to get there – people like me are told to get on the EXTREMELY delayed train to Aberdeen...

I don't want to go anywhere near Aberdeen today. And there's another catch: the Aberdeen train only has four carriages and now it's going to be full of Aberdeen-bound passengers plus a train load of additional passengers supposed to be on an entirely different train that no longer exists.

The need to become devious in these situations is extreme. You have to become extremely sneaky and obnoxious – ie take a first-class seat and smile like a crazy old lady having a secret piss in the ocean if challenged.

My particular happiness is that because I am on the road more than I am home, I have a particular attitude that allows me to cope when I see everyone around me sweating and trying to re-plan their ruined day – which never helps.

It pains me to see people almost cry with relief when they finally get on a train, thanking the train staff repeatedly as they squeeze in, not expecting or even caring at this point whether they'll get a seat.

All of this utter bullshit would be much easier to handle if you were paying 20p to be on the infernal thing in the first place. In all my years backpacking it never bothered me to have half a metal seat, to be seated next to a chicken or to be poked by a weird rusty iron bar sticking out where it shouldn't be, because the journey was cheap or free so what did you have to complain about?

Here you need a mortgage to buy a ticket for a train you know probably isn't going to show up and certainly isn't going to show up on time.

I kind of figure the same idiot running the NHS is also running the trains. The inefficiency is wild.

Then again, from a glass-half-full perspective, it does rather give me hope that the Net Zero mafia and the Green Militia will fail in their efforts to confiscate our cars. The very idea that the public transport network here in the UK would ever be good enough to replace the car is hilarious.

My American friends have never used a train in their lives. It is something they associate with the homeless, drunk or desperate people. But I have and I can confirm that their Amtrak service is a wonder and a delight. You can book a sleeper, get proper food, and it runs on time. At a tiny fraction of the cost we pay for our lack of service.

Same goes for the French trains: pretty ladies serve you lunch or coffee and the old idea of the glamour of rail travel somehow still exists.

Of the many solutions to save our railway, my money is on an asteroid.

APRIL

2 April

Mother and Father are not happy.

Inexplicably, they have booked themselves a cheap cruise around the Med. The cheap bit is perfectly explicable: they love a bargain, and nothing appeals to them more than the sense of having got a good deal. Given they are old, live in England and have cash to spare, why the hell shouldn't they book themselves a cruise?

The inexplicable part is that, as a couple who are not fans of people who eat their tea in front of the telly, they have booked a cruise with the very type of people who get on their tits.

Cruises are essentially floating prisons without the focus on rehabilitation.

I would bet my life that if something is marked down or on offer my mother would buy it. Even if she didn't need it, didn't want it and liked something full price better. The idea of a bargain is always too good for Grandma to refuse. Hence our cupboard being full of out-of-date biscuits, chocolates and most recently Battenberg cakes that no one in their right mind would buy even when they were still fit for human consumption, which was some three months ago now.

The trick to being my mother's good daughter is to be prepared to be a) supportive, b) certain it was a bargain, and c) enthused by whatever bargain the Mothership has sourced from the mean streets of Devon.

There is also the game of inverse haggling to be played. The rules are as follows:

1   The Mothership presents some fearful monstrosity that only someone off their face on ketamine would ever consider buying.
2   Mother will ask, 'Guess how much?' with the excited eyes of a predator that just caught a particularly fast-moving prey.
3   Regardless of whether or not you can see the charity shop label that clearly says £2.50, you must assume it came from a high-end store and guess exceedingly high in order to confirm Mother's all-time heavyweight champion status as the finder of the best bargains.
4   You say, 'Forty-five pounds!' and Mother replies, 'Two pounds fifty!' in a tone that infers you are a moron who can only hope to one day possess her special skills.
5   Everyone studiously avoids pointing out that what she has purchased belongs in a skip. Or landfill.

Mother presented herself to me the other day in an enormous, blazing-white Puffa coat – the sort of white that makes your eyes hurt if it catches the sunlight. It was 'oversize', as fashionable types like to say.

In truth, 'oversized' is an understatement. Mother is size 16 before we get started. Add to that an 'oversize' coat, layer on the 'Puffa' inflatable element, then imagine the whole gigantic thing in toothpaste white and you are getting close to the kind of monstrosity Mother, in her wisdom, saw fit to purchase. Basically a garment the size of an inflatable the likes of which you might hire for a kid's birthday party.

'Guess how much?' says Mum. It looks like her face is being swallowed by an iceberg. 'Guess!'

As stated, at this point in the game you have to guess high so that Mum can astound you with her exceptional bargain-hunting skills and convince you of how envious you should be, because you could never have got one yourself, such was the demand for this thing.

Given that River Island has taken money from my mother to turn her into an inflatable Eskimo, today I'm finding it hard to even muster up the strength to play.

'Ten pounds – ten pounds!' she crows, thrilled with herself.

I have a moment's thought about my drippy dogs and the fact they could do with a new duvet for their kennel... But I dutifully return to the situation at hand. It seems best to smile and nod and say it will be ideal for the cold. I can't help adding that perhaps she has enough coats and this one was a coat too far, even for her.

So now you know what we are dealing with, it will

not surprise you to learn the result of Mum and Dad enquiring about a cruise. In short, a 'lovely lady' from P&O telephoned them back and offered them 'a really good deal' and they are now booked on a two-week cruise around the Med. Inside cabin.

Mum and Dad have been around the Med more times than a ferry at this juncture, but there is something about the worry-free life on board (and the bargain) that appeals to them.

And I say do whatever makes you happy – but why not do it on Cunard? And why not get yourself a window? Or better still, a balcony?

The only way I would ever agree to get back on a cruise ship would be if I were guaranteed a balcony and a cabin as far away from the entertainment or kitchens as it is possible to be. Who in their right mind with disposable cash books an inside cabin? I am not rich, but the thought of being trapped inside with no window or fresh air makes me feel claustrophobic. Breathing other people's burps – or worse.

Still, you can't tell my parents.

I endured P&O's customer-service team to try and get them an upgrade out of my own pocket in order to make their experience somewhat more bearable, but after an hour waiting to speak to someone that identified as human I was informed that, regretfully, I could not pay to update my own parents because I was not the one responsible for the booking.

And even if I were I couldn't because there is an online

auction system for that sort of thing.

And even if I were successful in the auction I still couldn't because they had booked through a travel agent.

It makes you wonder, doesn't it? I am on the end of the phone with my VISA card, perfectly willing to hand over £600 or whatever it might take, yet I cannot persuade the woman employed by the company I want to pay money to, to take my cash.

15 April

Predictably, Mother disembarked her cruise raging at the hideousness of all the people on board. She rang to tell me that nothing had been right. I suspect this is a phone call all children of any age can relate to, regardless of what it is their mother needs to unload down the phone.

There were too many people everywhere. Too many people had too many children! The too-many children of the too-many people appear to have never been taught a single manner. And the too-many people and their children spent far too much time stuffing far too much food in their faces.

'And no one dresses up anymore!' exclaimed Mother, outraged that the grand old days of black-tie dinners on the Titanic with a full orchestra were not available on their bargain-basement Mediterranean cruise with the worst of mankind.

'As for getting off, well, I have never known anything like it!' she continued, in the tones of someone evacuated from their home in the dead of night and forced to sleep in a crowded Mexican slammer without a blanket or mattress.

After enduring the moan-athon, I texted my sister for clarity.

'Am I right in thinking Mother and Father just spent two weeks cruising around the Med, or were they sent to a Gulag on meagre rations for punishment?' My sister was surprised there had been any moaning left to do as she had already had an earful.

What a blessing it is to have old people in your life.

18 April

Possibly my very favourite thing about the spring, aside from the fact that all things are either mating, growing or springing forth in some jaunty manner, is lambs. There is NOTHING quite so wonderful as seeing a splendidly green grass field set against blue skies littered all about with little cottonwool fluff balls in ones and twos drinking milk from their reliable mother sheep.

Whenever I see them I feel genuinely thrilled for their little woolly hearts. They are so blissfully unaware of – everything.

Unaware that there is such a thing as winter lambing and that an entire field's worth of their sisters and brothers were born five months earlier. But instead of emerging to blue skies, jazzy green grass and the warm sun on their backs, these winter siblings were born into the freezing cold, lived in perpetual darkness and only ever knew rain before a lorry adventure that didn't end well and involved

Sainsbury's and mint sauce.

I would be so pissed off to be a winter lamb.

I remind myself that oblivion can be a very kind condition. Winter lambs are oblivious to the fact that there is such a thing as a spring lamb so have no sense of how badly they have been duped in this whole 'being a sheep' process.

That's before we get started on the myriad things to which the new winter lamb – we will call him Geoffrey – is oblivious.

Geoffrey has no idea that other animals get to live indoors, lie on sofas and get fed and walked twice a day and petted often. Geoffrey is in wonderful ignorance about the national governments being subsumed by a New World Order and, indeed, Geoffrey has never felt concerned that the level of Excess Deaths is at an all-time high.

So in many ways, despite being a winter lamb and having a bit of a shit existence compared to his spring counterpart, Geoffrey is free to focus on the important things in a new lamb's life, like finding mum and drinking milk.

Sheep are renowned for being one of the most labour-intensive animals on the planet to try and farm. If they aren't attaching themselves to barbed-wire fencing by their own eyeballs, they are falling on their backs and unable to right themselves again, like morbidly obese Americans at Disneyland. Unless someone comes to their aid they will die where they fall.

(I would make the argument that humans in this

predicament should be left to their fatty destiny given they have already made their life choices in front of the fridge / fast-food outlet.)

A flock of sheep can think of no better way to spend the hot months of summer than shitting directly into their own arse fur – providing an excellent nesting spot for a multitude of flies to lay their eggs in, and beginning the maggoty process whereby the sheep gets eaten alive arse-first.

If not impaled by its own eyelids or eaten arse-first by maggots, sheep have to be dipped in a large tank of strong-smelling chemicals to stop bits of their skin rotting off, dropping off or killing them in some other hideous manner.

And that's before you get to a sheep's feet, which fester in their own shit and piss for so long they develop abscesses that need lancing or spraying. And then they need shearing because their bastard great wool coats mean they overheat in the sun or get mud caked in the rain and threaten to kill them off in yet more special ways.

Sheep farmers are truly mental. They have to have sheep dogs just so there's one animal on the farm to restore their faith in the animal kingdom. They may have 2,000 head of sheep, but it's that one doggie that's going to keep them from blowing off their own head with a 12 bore.

In order for the winter lambs to arrive on the face of this planet, a mighty male sheep has to be put in with the ladies to plant the seed of his offspring up their sheep duff.

To check which ladies have been mounted, farmers

often attach a red dye dispenser to the underbelly of the male sheep – as he mounts the ladies he leaves a streak of dye behind to indicate that, with luck and a fair wind, they will be pregnant.

I've often wondered about the indignity of this – the male ejecting seed from his mighty erection and dye from the spray can attached to his balls, chalking up his conquests like a graffiti artist on the blank canvas of a sea of sheep rears.

I also see this from the lady-sheep perspective. One minute you're happily munching on grass, minding your own business and trying not to fall over because you might never get up again, and the next you're being royally rogered from behind without so much as a nice meal or a drink. And then, to add humiliation to sheep rape, you're spray-painted to prove that you submitted to the fat bastard who is still marauding about the field humping everything in sight.

Neither of them emerge well from the encounter.

Regardless, sheep are a royal pain in the arse and anyone who keeps them is a bloody saint. Or lives in a hilly place where you simply cannot keep cows. Or just never realised what a dreadful animal they are. Or spent too much time at Sunday school hearing a lot about shepherds and sheep.

Because sheep are one of the first things you learn about as a kid, right?

Q What did the shepherd watch?

A Their flocks by night.

The sheep were the ones who got to meet Angel Gabriel and hear all about the baby Jesus first.

It sets us up for a lifetime's belief that if we own sheep good shit will happen to us first. Then one day you find yourself trying to dip, shear, impregnate and herd the miserable fuckers and you realise you were conned.

Sheep are used in stories a lot to convey good and bad. Take this one from an enthusiastic pastor called Steve Dewitt. In his own words his story is rather long so I will summarise it for you. Do your best to stay interested to the end…

No one born of God makes a practice of sinning, for God's seed abides in him, and he cannot keep on sinning because he has been born of God. (1 John 3:9)

Christians may and will sin but it's no longer our nature to do so. We have a new nature, and by that nature we will not continue in what some call 'habitual and reckless' sin.

It's like the difference between sheep and pigs. Sheep and pigs get muddy and dirty. However, they view and experience it very differently. Sheep get muddy and dirty, but I don't think they like to. Their nature is different from the pig. The pig loves to get dirty and loves the mud. The pig is occasionally clean but prefers to be muddy. The sheep is occasionally muddy but wants to be clean. A pig will be happy to stay perpetually in mud. A sheep won't stay in the mud. It's not his nature to do so.

Now imagine that on the farm it rained for days and the pen outside the barn was a muddy mess. The mud was so thick and deep that one of your animals was stuck in the mud. Completely covered in mud. You actually can't tell what kind of animal it is. It's just a pile of mud with eyes looking out.

Days pass and you don't know what to do. The animal is still in the mud. So you call the veterinarian and you say, 'Doc, I have an animal encased in mud in the pen outside the barn. Can you help me identify it?'
He asks, 'What kinds of animals do you have there at your farm?'
You say, 'I have sheep and I have pigs.'
The vet asks, 'How long has this animal stayed in the mud?'
You say, 'He's been there for a week.'
'Well sir,' the vet says, 'I can tell you, it's a pig.'
'But,' you say, 'I talked with the animal and he told me he was a sheep.'
The vet says, 'He can say what he wants, but if he's been in the mud that long, there's no way he's a sheep, no matter what he says.'

No one born of God makes a practice of sinning, for God's seed abides in him, and he cannot keep on sinning because he has been born of God. By this it is evident who are the children of God, and who are the children of the devil: whoever does not practise righteousness is not of God, nor is the one who does not love his brother. (1 John 3:9-10)

Are you lost? Let me translate for you. No sheep makes a practice of staying in the mud; he's a sheep and cannot stay in the mud because he was born a sheep. By this it is evident who are sheep and who are pigs. Whoever stays in the mud is a pig.

Dear Christ Alive.

I am NOT for one moment saying that I am a gifted writer, but when I type you can hear my voice and you know it's me.

I am going to offer Pastor Steve some feedback – or 'feeeeeeeedback' as fat women from HR like to say (despite the fact they could do with a bit of feedback themselves). Pastor Steve, perhaps it is best you stay away from the computer and stick with the in-person preaching stuff. You look like a chirpy chap and I assume you will come across better that way.

I mean, you have to, because your writing couldn't be much worse. Writing like this is why our churches are empty and being converted into architect's offices or mosques.

His point, I think, if you were able to stay with him long enough to care, is that naughty types who sin a lot are like pigs and not at all Godly. But since we were all made by God and are God's little sheep, we only sin by mistake or accident. Or, in my case, when we see someone good-looking and hung like a donkey who is married to another women but we SIMPLY have to have him as our own.

(I am proud of myself for throwing in the idea Mark is hung like a donkey because donkeys are clearly Biblical creatures so this all works with the theme rather nicely.)

I fear I must reject Pastor Steve and therefore John 1

verse 3: 9-10 rather roundly on four counts:

1   I am capable of sinning quite a lot and certainly repeatedly.
2   And I enjoy it.
3   Pigs are way better creatures than sheep. I used to look after one at a pub and feed it scraps and beer each night and we got along very well.
4   Ever since the COVID 'pandemic' and the way other people were prepared to behave over the vaccines, I have been put off sheep-like behaviour forever. I will never forgive what the SHEOPLE were prepared to do to other humans like myself.

In fact, I would take an actual sheep, with a maggoty arse and a graffitied vagina, any day.

20 April

You will know by now I was never supposed to be a stand-up, or doing stand-up. I know I am funny and I make myself laugh all the time. I also know many people think I am an asshole.

However, as the world has got more mad, I'm aware that fewer people think I am an asshole and many more are realising that what they actually want to do is hang out and have a good time with other people who aren't trying to boss them about or belittle them. I am something of a performing monkey for these people and I'm thrilled to have the chance to be this person for however long they want me.

But let me tell you, for avoidance of doubt, it is not easy. It is very hard and marginally terrifying, which is why there aren't more people doing it.

It goes against every instinct of self-preservation to stand up in front of a crowd of people and say, 'I AM FUNNY!' – which is essentially what you're saying if you're trying to sell tickets for people to come and see you.

That's why so many comedians are big fans of selling workshop tickets, where they're working on their new material and finding out what is funny and what is not. Because the pressure is off and they have the chance to say, 'I could be funny, but I need your help.' Which is altogether more reassuring to the soul.

Now try being the 'I am funny' at Purfleet in Essex, in a massive great room full of people who know a good time when they see one. The last act before me was a local tribute to the Full Monty – essentially a group of well-oiled lads with massive cocks prepared to swing them about for a room full of rowdy women.

Right about now, backstage at this club, I envy them. How nice to know that your job is just to get on stage, get your kit off and rub your cock in someone's face. As a performer I think that would be a wonderfully reliable craft.

Purfleet in Essex has the stage at face-height for the punters, so those sitting at the front quite literally have their chins resting on the stage. This is marvellous if you are swinging your cock about and want to brush your nut sack along Linda's lips, or if you're a female performer and want to dangle your nipples into the face of Brian the builder.

But if you're 49-year-old me, uncertain if you have shaved your legs as well as you might have and with a varicose vein the size of a small anaconda on your shin, it's a bit disturbing. My tight trousers are not that forgiving and seeing my lovely crowd looking upwards from my ankles to my crotch sets me off in a direction unbefitting of a mother of three.

You will know, if you know me at all, that I am a wholehearted supporter of women and men who take their clothes off to earn a living. Be it regular prostitution, OnlyFans, nipples pointing to the sky at Hooters or erotic dancing – if you are safe and secure doing it, and it allows you to live your life, go you.

Upstairs at this venue in Purfleet is a gentleman's bar. And after my show it gave me a great deal of satisfaction to see hugely attractive girls making their way upstairs with a nod and a wink to the lads working security.

There's something about the working girls that I love. They are hugely attractive and fit as fleas, of course. But there is also something unrelenting about them, a toughness that is still kind, and a special resilience I am super drawn to.

I might think stand-up is frightening, but these girls do something far more exposing – getting their tits out is the least of it. They have to understand the men they are looking to please, spend time with them, give them what they are willing to transact, and secure enough tips and cash to make it all worthwhile. Now that's a skill and a talent not many girls are robust enough to sustain.

Best of all, when I was safely tucked into the car letting myself unwind under a blanket with a heated seat, Lovely Mark went back in to thank the staff and tip those who helped make the show possible. The security lads saw Lovely Mark coming and told him the owner was 'upstairs' and that he should head up to say goodbye.

Poor Lovely Mark hadn't seen all that I had seen, and was blissfully unaware… Right up until he was confronted by Beautiful Bella's Double DDs and Angel's pert little behind greeting him at eye level at the bar.

He came out of there looking like he was captain of the Good Ship Jolly Roger, in need of a stiff drink.

I am reminded that the road is the only place to be. All life is there.

MAY

'So why don't you just sod off to Tesco then?'

Possibly the least Waitrose thing I have ever heard, and fresh out of the face of Lovely Mark who had reached his quota for dealing with morons that day.

Predictably, not only is Lovely Mark quite lovely. And not only did he used to work at a donkey sanctuary, be kind to everyone and become the obsession of a great many women who see him and love him instantly. He also happens to be the wine guy at our local Waitrose store.

He keeps this entirely to himself; no one really knows except those who do. And he would be very happy to keep it that way. He is the 'wine guy' who the noisy members of staff in store wouldn't be able to place in a line-up. Most would say they had never seen him before, certainly never heard him speak.

Of course Lovely Mark is a wine guy. Despite coming from the wrong side of the tracks in Watford and growing up in a rough school where it was punch or be punched, Lovely Mark also knows how to fence, plays polo, and was a tennis coach. Sometimes I think he is the modern-day Zorro. He also skis like a bloody professional.

But that's not how all this started out.

After we were completely rinsed by the Powerful who decided my time was up, we needed to rebuild. Basic income, basic banking, basic home, basic everything. None of this could be linked to me in any way; I was unemployable – and always watched. Our only option was to effectively allow me to be killed off, and for Lovely Mark to find something we could rely on.

He became a night-shift worker at Waitrose, filling shelves from 10pm till 6am, along with a bunch of other lads who were desperate, disliked most of humanity, or were unable to tolerate the whims of demanding customers who believe their own poop smells like primroses.

For the longest time that's what Lovely Mark did: worked quietly through the night so he could still see the kiddies in the morning and then try and sleep (without success) until the next shift.

The pay would never have been enough to cover the costs of our little family, and the shifts were long – particularly around three in the morning, which I think is a bit like mile 18 of a marathon – but that's what Lovely Mark did in order to show that I wasn't responsible for everything and to make me feel less guilty about costing us everything we had, plus a great deal of what was rightfully his as well.

This is the remarkable gift of Lovely Mark. He's a bit like one of those deep-sea divers with the massive fins on their feet; he swims silently beneath me and somehow knows just the moment to lay all else aside and just quietly keep my face above the water until I can swim for myself again.

All the bastards sent to finish me are forcing my head under with their feet, but as long as Mark is there, unseen, I will make it.

As with all things to do with Lovely Mark, soon enough he was spotted at being really good at replenishing the wines. He speaks the language of bottles, and was able to replenish them faster than anyone else. And with more care and fewer breakages.

Working within the crazy system of Waitrose, with its extreme rules and processes and endless layers of management, Lovely Mark ended up working day shifts, with real-life customers. He sat his wine exams and jumped through the hoops to become The Wine Guy. He was given a Wine Guy apron to encourage customers to chat to him about wines.

This is not to suggest one thing is better than the other. It is not better to be The Wine Guy than to be The Poor Bastard Working the Nightshift Guy. I could not be more proud of him or any other mum or dad out there pulling nightshifts to make things work for their family. No one will understand the brutality of it, the leaving your home just as everyone is settling in their jimjams, or the coming home knackered when others are just about ready to face the day.

I think it is like a perpetual jet lag in its way of

disorientating you from all that you love. It is unspeakable.

But it is honest. And there are far fewer arseholes out at night than there are in the daytime. Old people are asleep. The workshy are asleep. And chunky women who like to boss people about much prefer to do that between the hours of 10.30am and 3.30pm.

Working the occasional day shift as The Wine Guy at Waitrose has presented a few problems on this front. For both him and me.

Let's talk about me first! Not that I have to insert myself into everything in the hope of getting some level of fuss or attention.

Lovely Mark is still a hottie. He's 60, could easily pass for 45 and is just as lovely as he seems at first sight. This has not escaped the attention of many of the exceptionally hot 50-year-old Waitrose customers who are through the menopause and ready to bang like a barn door but married to someone older, fatter and less attractive, who they last had sex with when leg warmers were still a thing.

These ladies are like bees on clover around the poor boy, offering up their ample charms to his bearded face in the hope that he might just nestle said bearded face against their unctuous boobies, even for a moment.

I have been one aisle over when a woman balanced a bottle in her ample cleavage and asked Lovely Mark to help her with her 'pronunciation'. This, I believe, is a euphemism for 'strip me naked and gobble me up like a turkey'. I considered grabbing an industrial roll of tin foil from aisle 4 and hammering her about the head with it.

Mark is undeterred by the hourly offers to bang women harder than a tight drum in the wine section, because he faces much greater challenges in the form of the average customer at his particular branch of Waitrose, set in the retirement county of Devon in an area of very rich boomers who made good when life still made sense.

I would like to say up front that I love old rock-and-rollers. I love old people who are weird and bonkers. I love old people who don't give a single shit and I simply can't get enough of the elderly who need a bit of help or want to be my friend.

But sadly, so few make the grade; a good 80% to 90% of our elderly go the other way.

I like to think of life as a tree – the tree of life. Each of us makes decisions throughout our life and each decision sets us off down a different branch. Some branches are spindly and half-hearted, but some of us make BIG choices that create thick main branches that come straight out of the trunk, change the trajectory of our own life and dictate the shape of the tree itself.

The big-branch creators are the mavericks, the mischievous imps, the delightful old people likely to land themself in need of rescue or at least strong coffee. The kind that are likely to shout 'FUCK YOU ALL!' in the middle of a church service and go off and watch taken men dancing instead.

My kind of old people.

The ones who took risky decisions. Made that crucial life choice to get on a boat and sail to a new country with a man they barely knew. Said yes to a job somewhere random that led to a whole new adventure in their lives. Got married eight times.

But so few do this!

The majority are so desperate to cling on to what they have, whether it be possessions or a life without risk, that that is all they ever achieve. They cling to the tree, make sensible decisions and barely notice as their whole life slips by.

Rich, old and protected from many of life's bruises, they are now both entitled and incredibly bored and frustrated at how small and unimportant they have become. They are the sort that still call themselves Major despite having left the army a full half-century ago, clinging to a time when they were saluted in the square.

Those are Lovely Mark's customers. Because wine and knowledge about wine have the glorious ability to make them feel 'better than' or somehow 'elevated'. It's an old snobbery – to know of wines and their origin, or to dictate what is 'good' or 'fine' is somehow up there with conversations about art or opera – conversations understood only by the educated classes.

This kind of snobbery is pure crap, I would argue (as I clutch my £5 bottle of Barefoot Merlot).

Regardless. For the embittered elderly, the wine aisle offers the opportunity to assert authority and power. Major Dick loves to parade about there, wearing his wine knowledge like medals.

Lovely Mark hasn't got much time for any of this, or

for the embittered elderly with nothing better to do than complain.

One grumpy git brought his wine back to the store complaining that it tasted corked. Mark explained that:

a   he had done pretty well to drink two-thirds of it if it was so awful, and

b   it had a screw cap.

Another demanded Mark's undiluted attention because the particular wine he wanted was cheaper in Tescos. Mark responded that he 'best get going to Tesco, then'. The grumpy old curmudgeon clearly realized he was not about to receive the apology and self-flagellation he expected from this particular John Lewis member of staff, and said as much.

'This is not the kind of response I would expect from a member of staff. I have a good mind to speak to your manager.'

Lovely Mark offered to go and get the manager for him.

And that's the wonderful thing about this time of life we are now in. I am able to work again and help cover the costs of our family. Lovely Mark still goes to work because we are grateful to his employers for being there when we needed a way to get by. But he knows that any day these miserable old gits get too much, or the stifling bureaucracy of 485 layers of John Lewis management becomes overwhelming, he can thank everyone kindly and walk out the door.

But for now, if you fancy flashing your cleavage at the

bearded guy in the wine aisle – that's Lovely Mark. Give it all you've got.

8 May

Today Charles became King and Camilla, his trusty sidekick, became Queen.

I should probably reveal my hand early on this one and confess that I am a big fan of Camilla. I think it's because she was so universally hated for so long that I have a natural kind of affinity for her. I also think her hair is brilliant and I suspect she would be a riot over a couple of G&Ts in the privacy of a good smoking bar.

You will know that the Hopkins band of ruffians is broad church, containing people from every walk of life with very different views on many things. Which is precisely the way I would have it. Some of our clan fervently believe the members of the Royal Family are all lizards, and the former Queen, Elizabeth, was the lizard leader.

In 1998 Time reported that former BBC reporter David Icke published a book called 'The Biggest Secret', which claimed members of the royal family 'are nothing more than reptiles with crowns'.

And it's not just monarchs who have been targeted with this scaly accusation. President Joe Biden has similarly been accused of being a reptile. In 2021 the BBC fact-checked a claim that a video existed that proved he wasn't human because a snake had been seen emerging from his jacket during a debate with then-President Donald Trump.

It wasn't, in fact, a snake but a rosary, which Biden wears to remember his late son, Beau.

I can't say I subscribe to any of this lizard-people stuff but I wholly respect the right of others to do so and do not seek to dissuade them from it. Although it's a challenge to be out there in front of a crowd and asked a specific question about whether I believe in lizard people; then I am forced to reply that this question is not really one for me, and falls outside my area of expertise.

But do I immediately get a spidey tingle when I am near a person of darkness? 100%. And do some people manifest as pure evil to me? Absolutely. I can even see how lizard people and people of pure evil might overlap.

It's interesting to me that those I immediately register as being pure evil never openly parade about as such. They are not illegal immigrants or young lads convicted of horrible crimes or serial killers or psychotics who do crazy stuff.

Pure evil always looks polished and wears a suit. It has mastered the art of being the most respectable person in the room. Which is completely lizard-like in nature – or chameleon-like, at least.

Regardless, Charles and Camilla did a splendid job of being made King and Queen and lots of our people watched on and had a lovely time of it, despite the pissing rain that totally kiboshed any street parties and plans for such. Charles must have wondered if this day would ever come, having so far lived a life totally about this moment. Little wonder he needed a sturdy bird who looks terrific at his side through all of it.

Lady Diana was epic in every way, of course, particularly in her revenge black dress, dancing with John Travolta or perched on the end of a diving board off a luxury yacht in the Med. My very favourite image of her ever was in her casual minefield-walking outfit: essentially chinos, a soft white blouse and excellent loafers.

I challenge any fashionista or influencer out there to look quite as good as Lady Di walking a minefield. Back at uni I longed to pull off such a look.

Angelina Jolie did try and replicate the whole affair when she was out and about paid for by the United Nations. She can always be relied upon to rock up pale and pouting with her mighty norks concealed under something modest.

That woman could cut cheese with her cheekbones. (Mine would struggle with marshmallow.) But even Angelina Jolie with her splendid cheekbones and mighty tits could never pull off what Lady Di managed to do seemingly without effort or premeditation.

Although I suspect behind all that fabulousness was a bit of a mental case with more issues than a daily newspaper. Making herself skeletal, chucking herself downstairs, looking mardy at the Taj Mahal, being interviewed by the serpents from the BBC – all this was never going to be tolerated by the Royals. And so they chucked her under a bus – or rather, squished her in a tunnel.

Few of us have any real understanding of the dark forces that operate to maintain the iron fist of power and control in our society. And few of us would want to. That's why so many prefer to live in a tiny bubble and keep their heads down and their eyes forward, as if life were Disneyland and the biggest challenge was getting to the front of the lines.

20 May

I am pretty certain the news that the long-beaked echidna is not extinct after all is helping power you through the month of May. Echidnas are those weird creatures that look a bit like hedgehogs whose spikes have grown way longer than they should, are closely related to dinosaurs, and, in a bonkers twist, still lay eggs. Perhaps this is because of their fishy origins. (I say that, and then remember that chickens, too, lay eggs but are the least fishy-looking animal you could imagine.)

In case you are interested in the details, there are four different species of echidna, some of which have long beaks and some short. The Attenborough echidna and the western echidna are considered critically endangered.

Either way, the BBC is very excited about it. Here's how they broke the news to their dedicated audience that said echidna had been found alive and well:

'Named after the nation's favourite natural historian and broadcaster, the Attenborough's long-beaked echidna (Zaglossus Attenborough) was thought to have fallen into extinction. But now University of Oxford researchers have not only spotted this rare creature in Indonesia's Cyclops Mountains, they were able to film it as well.'

As debating types like to say in the chamber, I have a few points of order on all of the above.

Firstly, the phrase 'nation's favourite natural historian and broadcaster' is a bit of an over-reach. Back in the day when good old David marauded about in jungles taking grainy footage of gorillas, I think the consensus was that he was a jolly good egg. I held this view for much of my life, certainly well into my 30s.

But in more recent years David has become the most almighty bore. Despite being feted with massive budgets and entire countries-worth of camera crews and experts, we cannot get a single video of a flamingo, turtle, snake, penguin or feathered something without an infernal lecture on climate change or man-made hell.

David has become a doom-monger and a missionary for those determined to force guilt into our lounges via the TV.

Attenborough no longer brings us the sort of amazing animals that make us want to go out immediately and pick up litter to make things better. He has to show us images of baby sealions being suffocated by fishing trawlers. And it's a rum affair.

If I wanted to be in tears of an evening, I would watch a sad film. If I am watching something called Blue Planet, that's exactly what I want to watch. Fishy things being fishy. Or weird bastards at the very bottom of the deepest trench ever explored with one eyeball on the end of a stinging tentacle and 18 penises in their own mouths. That's the shit I want my taxes to fund.

Back to today's bulletin and the BBC writer is casually referring to Oxford researchers in Indonesia's Cyclops Mountains.

As if they just rocked up in the Cyclops Mountains in Indonesia on a Monday morning, as you do, just looking for echidnas. Or maybe not even looking, just stumbling on them by chance. But you know, good people, these 'researchers' are not there on their own dime. This isn't a self-funded solo-adventurer kind of trip. This is your taxpayer cash, funding some over-educated lunatics to stumble about in far-away mountains documenting spiky animals thought to have disappeared from the planet a few hundred years ago.

What do you think would happen if you put any of these over-educated Doctor Dolittles behind a check-out till at ASDA and asked them to work an eight-hour shift with the general public? I genuinely think their heads would explode, leaving grey matter all over the multipack garlic bread.

The last thing I want to say before never mentioning the word echidna again, or Attenborough for that matter, is that to say something is extinct is a MASSIVE assumption, as this spiky little critter has proven.

How can some corduroy-wearing naturalist geeks decide a species is extinct? Just because they haven't seen one rocking about for a few years – just because that little swarm of flying things or herd of furry things isn't where you saw it last – that's not a good enough reason to shout about extinction and try to get people to drive stupid battery cars, is it?

The world is a bloody big place. There are huge bits of it that are uninhabited – half the sea floor is a mystery, and there are entire land masses that are left well alone. Is it not possible that some of these 'extinct' species have found solace where humans are not?

And is it not also possible that species no one has ever heard of are living their best life without mankind studying them, or trying to misguidedly 'protect' them, or some over-privileged boarding school kid whose parents have too much cash spending a gap YAAAAR pretending to look after their eggs?

It all feels like a pantomime to me and I am no longer buying a ticket. If I want to see something furry I will stand in a field and if I want to see birds I will look up a tree. And if I really feel the need to see a fish, I will go sit by a river.

Attenborough and his scare-mongering climate-change pushers can sticky their spiny echidna up their arses.*

(*If Attenborough dies during the publication process, be clear: I don't apologise and I don't retract a word. Death does not make one immune from criticism. See the way Thatcher was treated for details.)

26 May

I nearly hit a cyclist on my way home today.

I am not sure if I am disappointed that I missed, or slightly relieved that I am not in custody being charged with manslaughter. My only defence would be that 'he had it coming, yer honour', which in fairness he did.

I cannot fucking stand cyclists.

I cannot stand their perky little Lycra outfits. I cannot stand their disgusting calves all bulgy and sinewed. And I cannot stand their bastard attitude.

As for the ones with a camera on their head, whenever I see one I fervently wish for an American baseball bat with which to take a bloody good swing and separate their head from their scrawny little excuse of a body.

Cyclists are vinegar and lemon all wrapped up in a bitter walnut skin.

And their attitude stinks. Encouraged by lefty morons and funded with enormous salaries by the likes of the BBC, they get subsidies for their fucking bikes, cycle paths to bomb about on, and private places to securely lock their expensive bits of kit. And they are encouraged to get in the way of motorists and taxi drivers trying to earn a wage.

If you are in doubt about just what monumental dicks these idiots are, please look on the John Lewis website where they are selling something called Le Col Pro Bib Cycling Shorts for £185.

Who has £185 to spend on cycling shorts that go over your shoulders? And why the fuck does your average posh twat on a bike need to wear a lycra onesie for a half-hour cycle? It is pure sexual perversion.

When our local Peloton is out on the roads it takes all my willpower not to smash into them like a crazy Jihadi at a Christmas market shouting, 'Fuck you all, you puny bastards!' I'd be tempted to reverse back over them as well to check I'd finished them off.

I can't quite explain the deranged rage I feel about cyclists or how close I come, at least in my mind's eye, to carrying out acts of vengeance. I think it comes from the certainty that the people on these festering bikes are a concentrated form of all the things I most dislike, and to be rid of them would be a blessing.

In a rather more moderated tone, I also question where the hell their dicks are. When one of them is doing their wanky 'I'm a cyclist wearing clip-on shoes' walk to get his frigging double espresso, I sometimes take the chance to have a look. And there is NEVER anything there. Not once have I met a well-hung cyclist.

Either men with small dicks are attracted to cycling, or cycling appeals to those who have been blighted by a lack of sexual experience and prowess... and therefore fun.

Their tiny cocks achieve what you might think to be the impossible, namely to make me like them even less.

I wish them nothing but massive piles and pissing rain. And the odd pothole they don't see until it is too late. Film that, you bunch of c*nts.

JUNE

4 June

'You alright, Mum?'

That's codespeak right there. That's my daughter asking, 'Why are you being a major-league stress? Calm the fuck down, why don't you.' Without saying it.

More annoying than the codespeak itself is the fact she is right. I am A LOT sometimes and I suspect one of those times is now.

This is going to sound like an excuse but I think you will relate. Sometimes in my overwhelming need to get everything done all at once, to clear the truly mammoth shit-storm that sits in a catchment area between my work, my home and the many living things that depend on me, I just need to exert massive energy.

I've come to see it as volcano-level power, or that shock wave you see in movies after a nuclear strike, the one that blows across kilometres, flattening everything in its wake. That's me when I feel out of control and need to get everything back under control at speed.

I move through the house like an angry Ukrainian body-builder with thrush, and woe betide anything that gets in my way. I empty bins as I pass, vacuum floors on my way to unload the washing machine, and post content with a mop up my arse as I simultaneously mop the bathroom floor.

Anyone who gets in my way knows they will be given a job, so they run for cover like rabbits when the lions are on the prowl. The look of misfortune on the face of whichever teen gets caught! They know their best bet is to say, 'Yes Mum,' and just get that shit done.

Storm Hopkins is now unstoppable. Not only am I doing 18 hours-worth of clearing up everyone else's shit in 60 minutes – I am also the self-appointed judge and jury about how hard or not the other individuals in my house are working.

I am the ultimate grafter, the worker bee, the unrelenting provider, and everyone in my path will be judged by me and found wanting. Little Max is clearly guilty of not being able to see an obvious job that needs doing even when it is in front of his face. Lovely Mark clearly needs sentencing for spending too long behind his Mac tippy-tapping out emails. And Indy Windy has no right to breathe in this house because she is 19.

Right now I hate everyone. And hoolie-doolie, am I going to let them know about it.

I can maintain this nuclear-level fission for around three hours, sighing and huffing and puffing as I offload my EXTREME ANGER and let everyone know they are complete lazy bastards and I am the only one who does anything in this house ever.

I'm fuelled by the insane, abject levels of laziness I discover as I travel about in my cleaning frenzy: three nearly-used toilet rolls on the floor near the toilet bin, because it was easier, presumably, to start a new one than to finish one off. Toothbrushes never placed back on charge, now leaving revolting little black rings on the sink. Top drawers filled with wrappers of shit presumably eaten in bed in the middle of the night. Or, my particular favourites, the almost-empty tube of toothpaste and bottle of shampoo that no one can be arsed to coax the last bit out of.

It's not like my bastard kids were brought up with cleaners or with a silver spoon in their gob. They know it is just me, and they know a little bit about the pressure I put myself under. But somehow their time still matters more than mine.

If the vacuum cable gets knotted in my efforts, or something bangs and crashes to the floor making even more mess, then watch out, because the language that follows is not pretty. And if ANYONE tries to do anything in this nuclear moment, be it eat, shit, lie down or take off a sweater, they can be sure as the sun rises that I will be up their arse like a prostate exam asking them passive-aggressively to clean up after themselves as they go.

I do all of this with a face like a slapped arse, my triple chins wobbling in the wind, my hair the love child of a bag lady and a greasy spoon, clad in leggings with a slightly whiffy crotch area, topped by an old sweater.

Much later, when I am sat with a glass of wine, cheese and crisps, I can see I was not a good person during these moments. By the time everything smells of bleach and there is no shit to be seen anywhere, I sometime feel a bit regretful about having been that monster. I try and quietly make up for it by being a bit nice.

I suspect the truth is many of us go to this place at least once a week: hating everyone you are related to, vowing that one day you will walk out and go live in a gorgeous apartment that smells of Jo Malone and beeswax, wondering how the fuck everyone else gets to have it so easy.

Once the red mist has cleared, we remind ourselves that we wouldn't be without our family. If I was single with none of these lunatics around me, I would wonder what the hell I had done with my sad little life, to have no one to share it with me. I remember the times when I was a single mum of two under two, and how I would drive to Tesco just to have somewhere to go with the girls where I wouldn't be judged for having small people and also wouldn't be so desperately alone.

I am learning to reflect on this kind of behaviour now that I am approaching 50. I'm not saying I am changing it any time soon, but I am confessing that I see myself doing it. Nevertheless, although it is not particularly pleasant for my family, perhaps it is needed. Like a vent in a volcano or a lance in a boil. If I don't let all this pressure out in a relatively controlled situation inside my home, I might self-detonate in public. And in the age of a camera in every pocket, that feels like a very bad idea indeed.

16 June

My online pub, the Katie's Arms, is jollying its way along very nicely at this point. At 8pm on Friday here in the UK I spend 30 minutes LIVE on Insta, chatting away as if I'm in a pub back in the good old days when we could just hang about in bars and drink and smoke and chat to anyone.

I started the pub during lockdown when I could feel the huge weight of human sadness and loneliness and I had to do something to try and fix it. And somehow, laughing at the madness was a kind of therapy for myself and many others.

My only hope for the pub is that it is a place where people can laugh with me or at me, or to talk about whatever anyone fancies.

More importantly, those 'in' the pub online can see others also in the pub joining from America, Canada, Mauritius, South Africa. And that's the true beauty of the thing. It allows people to see for themselves that they truly are not alone.

About 5,000 people join in at some point over the half hour and a further 50,000 or so catch up afterwards. It's best not to think about what this number would actually look like in a room, nor is it realistic to do so as an online viewer is very different to the type of person who goes out of their way to attend a gig in person.

There is no reason for me to do the Katie's Arms. It's not for financial gain, as there is no money element involved, but it's not purely for my own entertainment, although clearly I have a need to be needed, to put it politely.

It's not for self-promotion, either. Getting my arse in front a camera at 8pm on a Friday is not always the thing I entirely want to be doing.

But it does give me the discipline of performing and of testing out ideas that pop into my head under pressure.

In truth, I get a heap of lovely emails and comments, mainly from ladies around my age who feel that the Katie's Arms keeps them sane, and it makes them laugh and feel better about themselves. Some are generous enough to credit me with getting them through the last four years or so of the madness. I suspect I have played only a small part, but that's good enough for me.

So we get together, I have my bottle of Barefoot and a wine glass handy, and I rattle through some things I think might be interesting or that have just happened in my life – much like this book.

Regulars know what to expect. They can laugh along or just tune out – they might even ask the odd question or get a mate to join us.

Newcomers are shocked for any number of reasons. Their most common comment is, 'Clearly Katie had a few drinks before opening the pub doors.' Or, from complete outsiders, 'Holy cow, how drunk is this woman?'

I've spent a lot of time thinking about this.

Those that know me well know that I would never

knowingly put myself into the public eye when shitfaced. I don't drink before I open the pub doors or go live.

There's no way I would have the brain speed to rattle through the stuff I'm talking about if I were three sheets to the wind. But these facts are not the point.

The point is that to the ordinary outsider looking in, who don't me, who were probably in the middle of doing something else, stumbled across me by accident and have no clue what the hell is going on – the best explanation those people can come up with about me is that I am drunk.

What's so interesting about this is their need to explain me away.

The outsider looking in needs to somehow package me up as something they can understand. Why is this older woman dressed like a whacky old bat laughing away to herself while saying stuff she really shouldn't?

To make themselves feel more comfortable, they actually take the time to type the words, 'Christ, how much has this bird been drinking?'

There are two things that I am certain of, and one of them is deadly serious.

The first is that I can be like I am at the pub because my job is to bring the energy that allows others to relax – totally relax. Because I openly overshare about my affairs, or my piles, or my disasters in the crotch department, others feel able to let their guard down.

So I take the piss out of something you shouldn't, or gob off about how Kate Garraway totally grifted off long

COVID (on the day after her husband died), or do my impression of Stephen Hawking on Epstein's island. I've laughed on there, I've cried on there, and I've showed off my hairy legs. There is no filter, no apology and no effort to pretend to be something I am not (though I do my face and hair before I rock up and I have lights that make me look way better than I do in real life).

The thing about social media is that all the rest seem to be out to prove they are better, brighter, more successful or more in control of their lives than you.

There's the perfect-pants housewife showing how tidy her frigging closet is or how best to fold a fucking pair of jeans (give me strength). You have exceptionally hot young men doing nothing more than grinning into camera and flopping their floppy hair about. (Yes, you're cute. Now go meet real girls.) And then you have plump young things trying to flog make-up or clothes or skin care to people hoping it will make them feel better about their own life.

Not forgetting the over-privileged cockheads that need to share their luxury holiday so they can feel validated about how well they are doing and how happy they are – sitting in the Maldives checking on clicks and likes from their adoring fans stuck at home in chilly England.

If you ask me, that's the behaviour people should be worried about. Not me sat in my little office with a glass of wine in my hand.

Regardless, being an open door for others to walk through and to feel better about themselves is a gift and a pleasure and I love the positivity of it all.

The second, much more serious point jars with all of the above.

This year we have been witness to something that doesn't sit right with me at all – and it is the deaths of multiple women in rivers. These have been explained by the police as 'unfortunate incidents' in which women (of about my age) 'enter the river' and then drown.

I am not trying to be an armchair detective. I have no experience of anything to do with rivers and I am certainly not wanting to interfere or inflict more sadness.

But my heart tells me that none of these things are true. I don't believe these women simply 'entered the water'. I don't believe their deaths are just 'unfortunate'.

Women like Nicola Bulley, 45, who police denounced as a drunk in the days after she went missing, her dog still frantically scratching about in the place he last saw her, and her phone left neatly on the bench where she had been sitting. That lovely lady had managed to get herself together, to get her daughter ready and off to school, to begin a dog walk in the park and hop on a teleconference all before 9am in the morning – and what? The world is told to shrug because some lazy policewoman uses the term 'drinking issues'?

Or Gaynor Lord, 55, leaving her job at a department store to rush rush rush towards a local park. I know that run – leaving work before you should, rushing to put your coat on as you go, even though it would be quicker to stop and sort it properly, excited for something, excited about something. She was supposed to have neatly folded her glasses and placed them with her phone and then 'entered the river'?

I may not know these ladies in person, nor their personal stories. But I know ladies like Gaynor, full of movement and verve, don't decide to take a dip in a cold river on a dark November evening.

There are others: mum of three – missing; married mum of two – body in river... The list seems to go on. So odd, so out of character and yet so simply brushed away, tidied up like crumbs under the toaster, as if they are things of every day, too mundane to hold anyone's attention.

Many ladies will understand the weird feeling of being invisible. Obviously, it's a bit different for me in places where I am a bit known. I am a good old cow and blessed that strangers come up and give me a hug or say hello. But in countries where I am not known, I too am invisible. Not just because I am a foreigner, but because of my age.

I see it when I walk with my daughters. I see the eyes of men and of boys. I watch butchers behind their counter looking when they think I don't see, I see the garage lads, fixated. I see it in the street. I remember it from when I was young, and I see how it passes like a baton to the newer, younger, more fabulous things.

This is nature's way, and a good thing too.

But the side effect is that invisible women of 50 don't count when they go missing in a river. Or fail to come home after walking the dog. Or when their phones or clothes or dogs are found near a river. The ready assumption is that they entered the water of their own volition and that was the end of that.

No struggle for life, no effort to self-preserve, even though that's what a great many women are doing on a daily basis just to keep it together for the sake of their kids, or the sake of their marriage, or the sake of their parents, or everyone else's sake but their own.

It may be over-sensitive of me. It may be a long leap from someone calling me drunk because they see me being free and happy on my social media feed. But the dots line up for me as clearly as stars on a chilly night sky without clouds.

These subtle acts of dismissal are indicative of a much harder truth, a truth that belies the integrity of the 'equality' conversation. Relatively young women, at 50 or so, are in the no man's land of life.

These women give life to the new and sustain and nourish them. These women are the fantastic ordinary, who anchor us and weave us into the fabric of something. These are the women who make the world go round – and yet these women are left to fall in the shadows without anyone being there to catch them.

We are all Nicola and Gaynor and the rest. We should all feel uneasy at the thought they could have been saved.

28 June

Sir Elton is playing at Glastonbury this year. Not that you'd recognise the place if you went now. Twenty years on from when I was last there it is unrecognisable.

I woke up in my tent at Glasto alongside my mates and

an additional snoring person none of us knew. We lay there for a while in the sweaty smelliness of it all, mouthing at each other, 'Who the fuck is that?' But none of us knew. Or particularly cared.

I was there in the good old days when the brave and /or impoverished could still jump the fence at personal risk and get in for free. My mate Julie did exactly that to great acclaim. Sadly, her sidekick made the grave error of jumping with her rucksack on her back, fell awkwardly and fractured her thigh bone.

The toilets were beyond vile. I considered myself well-versed in the worst humanity had to offer by the time I hit the Glasto toilets aged 19, but I remember being paralysed in the heat of the blue cubicle at the sight of a mound of human poop that piled up over the top of the seat, topped by a light sprinkling of jizz where a man of uncertain upbringing had found himself inexplicably turned on by the faecal pile and bashed one out over it all.

That wanked-on poop at Glasto is seared onto my retinas for all time. It has become what the over-zealous on Instagram call a core memory (although they tend to apply it to something joyful, like a boy meeting his new puppy dog for the first time, or a child surprised by his father coming home from deployment).

I have never taken drugs other than those injected into me by a paramedic or surgeon, or inhaled deeply from a hospital tank of gas and air, but I am of the view that Glasto is probably one of those experiences in life that is much improved by some kind of substance abuse. This is certainly true for cancer and death. Or even divorce, now I come to think of it. And childbirth. And maybe sex.

What we are learning here is that many things in life are better with the addition of drugs and Glasto is certainly one of them. (I am starting to wonder if all life wouldn't be better with substance abuse; maybe that explains my relationship with Merlot.)

That is not to suggest I behaved myself at Glastonbury; 'all evidence to the contrary,' as my father exclaimed when it was discovered that I had contracted scabies and impetigo simultaneously. I don't like to think about how I got infected or infested, but whereas most people come away with memories, I came away with contagious afflictions. The scabies ate away at the skin between my fingers and in the creases of my eyes and neck. The impetigo cascaded down my face in a constellation of pustules, each more painful than the last.

If a West End production of Oliver Twist had needed a new scabby washerwoman, I'd have been a shoo-in.

Undaunted, I continued to show my face in public working as a bar maid and the men I served seemed not to be the slightest bit put off by the fact the young girlie handing them their beer was covered in mites and boils and was almost certainly contagious.

These days Glastonbury is so changed as to be unrecognisable. Gone are the swathes of students from dodgy polytechnics and the grass-munching original vegans without much to their name. Gone are the tent crashers and the randoms. Glasto has been gentrified in the most depressing of ways, along with everything else inside its now fortress-like walls. Tickets are £250 plus, chips cost as much as a posh coffee and pints are £10 a pop.

We knew the poshos had officially arrived when Jeremy Corbyn made it to the main stage, but in subsequent years the Arabella quotient has multiplied and now all the poshos and their posh kids 'do Glasto' together, en masse, in the same way they 'do' the Courchevel ski season or Cornwall.

For them it is 'such fun' to be 'doing' a festival, and they get to play dress-up in what they imagine to be festival-chic, which involves buying a whole new, predictable wardrobe of jangly bracelets, floaty skirts and the odd hair braid or butterfly face sticker.

What comes first I wonder, the twat or the money? Is it their money that makes them twats, or are they twats at birth and their money just amplifies their twattery?

Probably a combination of the two. And because money likes to stick around money, they are surrounded by their own kind, encased in a kind of twat cocoon that enables them to continue behaving like twats completely unchecked.

Sir Elton was on stage this summer. He said it was his very last-ever performance at a UK festival, and therefore part of his farewell tour for his fans. I think Elton has had about three farewell tours to date, so you can take it with a pinch of salt.

If he gets short of a few bob or needs another hair

transplant, he'll be back performing 'I won't let your son go down on me' at some gay club in Soho. Or, more likely, at some fundraiser for the newly divorced former Prince known as Harry.

30 June

What is with our local police and sitting in lay-bys like massive perverts trying to catch people speeding? What are they doing in those vans inbetween taking pictures of a car doing 43 in a 40mph zone? Is it a game to them? Do they laugh when they catch someone?

Because I don't find it or them the bloody slightest bit funny.

I wonder what would happen if I stopped my car in front of one of these mobile speed camera vans and started giving these tiny little chipolata cocks inside a piece of my mind. I have been wondering this for quite a little while now and, knowing me, there will come a point when the red mist descends and I go right ahead and do it.

What in God's name do these police 'men' think they are doing?

They know exactly where to position themselves: either at the foot of a hill where you are naturally accelerating, just after an uphill dual carriageway where you have needed to speed up to get past a lorry, or tucked in behind a frigging tree during a holiday or big family-travel weekend.

I truly believe these freaks get a weird semi on from catching ordinary people just about 'breaking the law' (if you subscribe to the idea of a bonker's law in the first place).

I couldn't do it, I wouldn't do it, and having survived being a cleaner, a security dude, a fast-food girl and an assortment of other menial roles, I can say hand on heart I would rather do anything honest than sit in a car policing others who are just going about their business.

It's typical of the crap policing we see all over the place. It is so much easier to police people who are mostly operating within the law and trying their best to comply with an ever-expanding list of regulations. It is so much harder and more challenging to police the malevolent fuckers that thieve, pimp, push drugs or sell weapons.

Which is why only 1 in 20 crimes in this country ever sees someone caught and prosecuted and why crime definitely does pay.

There is NOTHING police in Scotland like better than a bit of on-line policing. How lovely to pass your day being paid to sit on your arse reading a few tweets and sending some goons round to knock on doors in the name of 'hate speech'.

Never mind that just down the road Ahmed is operating a money-laundering business and running drugs and AK47s all over Bradford. As long as some white guy called Terry gets his knuckles rapped for calling a rival football team supporter a black twat – even when this description is entirely accurate.

You should see the responses I get to this kind of rant from those involved in policing decent people or the idiot goons sent to break up freedom rallies or our occasional protests.

The goons in questions will argue, 'I'm just going my job.'

That's going to be a firm no from me, just so we are clear.

If you are willing to do the bidding of tyrants, you are one. No one gets a free pass to cosh other humans, to corral them into places they don't want to be, to hold innocents against their will, or to enforce rules that are clearly irrational.

If you do that you are not 'just doing your job' – you have become the long arm of their reach and the very thing we need to push back against.

Look into the mirror. Can you stand what you see? Can you tolerate what you do? Is it honest hard work intended to improve life generally? Is it in the best interest of ordinary people just like yourself? If the answer is no, you might want to rethink your choices.

I ask 'police' who sit in their car trying to sting families with a speeding ticket when they are just trying to drive away to get a break together, how do you look at yourself in the mirror? How are you happy earning your wage? Is it okay to fine others because it means you yourself will never get a fine?

I prefer a burglar to your sort. At least a thief is honest about the fact he is stealing from you and does it while your back is turned.

You – the police – are the issue. I think you should

reconsider what you are doing for a living. I think you should do something more worthwhile. I firmly believe you know what you are doing is wrong.

You may be able to justify it in your head by telling yourself lies. You can tell yourself public safety is improved because your jackass is sat in that lay-by catching people speeding. But that's just spooning yourself medicine to avoid the uncomfortable truth.

I spit every time I see your cars.

Come and work on our side – farming, building, writing, maintaining, scaffolding, mending, mining, selling – the side that simply wants everyone to get along and to be as free as they can be.

JULY

I sense the greenie maniacs are never going to let this drop... It's been above 20 degrees in the UK for at least three days on the trot and already the TV weather goons are screaming at us about death and dehydration, stabbing at maps largely coloured red or black.

Something very odd has happened to map-colouring that we haven't been told about. When I was young, sunshine was yellow or orange, reassuringly slapped on to a magnetic map by a bird with equally magnetic tits.

You must remember, 'Scorchioooooo..!' Weather girls in the Med had the most piss-easy job because every damn day was hot and for most of the year all they really needed to say was, 'Scorchio' – which is the kind of weather I can really get behind.

Then came the age of technology and whizzy screens designed to let us see the actual weather that was being forecast. We would ooh and ah at the graphics as they rolled by like those 'plot your path' screens on airplanes.

Then, in a weird twist we should have seen coming

given the trajectory of modern society, a plethora of nattily dressed gay male weather presenters sprang up in ever tighter suits and shorter trousers. Barely a forecast goes by without a gay presenter dude with a regional accent, sporting trousers designed to create a focal point of the crotch area, slip-on loafers and no socks.

Inversely, the women got a whole lot less attractive. The job of the weather girl (and this is still the case in the US) is to look as hot as possible while delivering weather bulletins men never hear because they're too distracted by the display of tits. The side profile of a weather girl is particularly crucial; the upper-body silhouette should be plump but also perky, and suggestive of a jolly good time to be had whatever the forecast.

These hotties, like the one Lovely Mark obsessed over for a while, delivered the weather with a tight top, perky tits and a caressing hand. All over the country, men sat beside their wives on the sofa and imagined Miss Perky fondling their balls.

How things have changed. Nowadays British weather girls are sturdy beasts who have calved half a herd and the only thing expanding is their waistline and the size of their brood.

Trying to listen to the weather delivered by one of these wildebeests is distracting, and not in a good way, not to mention that half of Wales is obscured by their fat arse.

Returning to the weather charts... In what seems like a retrograde step down the evolutionary path, we are back to some kind of colouring-by-numbers whereby the happy yellows and oranges have been replaced by blood reds and foreboding blacks, as if to indicate that the end of the world is nigh. Or, as the head of the United Nations has suggested, we are at the point of 'climate boiling'.

The United Nations is a pointless organisation at the best of times. My friends in Israel call it the United Nothings due to their preference for being united in doing absolutely bugger-all as they watch ordinary people being raped, slaughtered or both – though usually consecutively, not concurrently.

When the head of said useless organisation starts coming out with the kind of climate hysteria we are growing so tired of, I happen to think more people are turned off than inspired to take action.

This kind of massive hyperbole is wrong on so many levels.

Firstly, I think it has a vaguely hypnotic effect on the legion of young people who have been indoctrinated into believing the end of the world is nigh due to cow farts and cars, and who are convinced they are doomed – and, worse still, doomed to death by boiling, like a frog in a pan, except that they were the smart frog that realized all along what was coming.

For these gloomy doomsayers, the head of the UN with his global boiling is only confirming what they have already been brainwashed into believing.

What point living if not to take action against this wilful 'genocide'? What point childbirth if the world is about to end? What point working when life itself is futile?

What point building or caring or mending or supporting when it's each man for himself as the Titanic goes down?

In a world that is ending, gluing yourself to a picture or concreting your hands to the tarmac actually makes sense because nothing else does...

Hyperbole like 'global boiling' leads to more of this kind of mentality.

If we are all boiling to death anyway, the climate situation is 'out of control' and annihilation is inevitable then, for these young cultists, there is no point in anything. The Titanic is certain to sink, they have always known this was their fate, and there is no point at all in trying to board a life raft. They might just as well go rearrange a deckchair and listen to the orchestra – or, in their terms, go to Glastonbury, get shitfaced and still find time to glue themselves to something or other, or spray paint something orange.

Which is precisely what happened this year. After Glastonbury the posh kids returned to spraying banks and other corporates orange, and disrupting racing, football and Wimbledon. At Wimbles the thundercunts released orange glitter bombs. Surely they know Ralph Lauren hates orange?

And on and on it goes. The climate cultists veering increasingly into freakish cult behaviour that makes WAKO look positively sane. Those of us who would just like to live a bit more kindly and cleanly, to help look after fish or furry things, are endlessly punished for trying to live, eat, breathe or even shit.

And God help you if you want to drive. Those days are surely numbered.

Wales is a perfect example – and that's not something you'll hear said about Wales very often.

The guy busy running the place into the ground would make Xi Jinping proud, with his militant approach to rules and regulations and his sheer determination to crush the fun out of everything.

Like many other communist hubs – Toronto, Melbourne, Portland, California – Wales had one of the most draconian lockdowns on the planet. The Welsh were kept in a constant state of befuddlement and scrutiny thanks to the never-ending list of rules they were obliged to adhere to.

Layer upon layer of irrational decision-making made life in Wales like trying to find shelter under a flimsy construction of playing cards, most of them jokers.

You were allowed to buy essential items like vodka and cigarettes. You were not allowed to buy essential items like children's clothes or lightbulbs.

I would argue – strongly – that vodka and cigarettes are indeed absolutely essential items in Wales. I would go so far as to say it is probably not possible to get through a week in Wales without either drinking heavily or smoking so hard you pass out.

Those of you who have been around my bonkers life for a while will know that I used to have a delightful Welsh boyfriend called Jonathon. It turns out the gorgeous man was actually gay and using me as a cover – I think the term is a 'beard' – for his family, who all lived in Merthyr Tydfil. When I say they all lived in Merthyr, I mean they all lived in one street in Merthyr, mother next to aunt across from brother and just down the road from uncle. Just like in Gavin and Stacey.

They were all delightful and gorgeous; Jonathon was, too. I just genuinely hadn't realised he was gay, though I did wonder why my obvious sexual charms were lost on him. I like to think I was a helpful part of his life back then, and I'm still cheering him on now.

He also taught me valuable lessons about not being a backwater hillbilly and how to grow a decent gaydar, which I now have every faith in. When a gorgeous boy announces 'I'm gay' to me these days, I say, in the manner of an aged theatrical dame, 'But of course you are, daaaarling!'

But Drakeford's madness was seemingly neverending.

He even slept in his garden shed during this period in order to isolate his family from his germs (walking, as he was obliged to, among the ordinary people). I think this was a Christ-like move on his part, spending 40 days and 40 nights in the wilderness alone, suffering to test his faith.

Drakeford the Communist Jesus spent three months sleeping next to the lawnmower and the Black and Decker hedge-trimmer in order to protect his wife, who was shielding.

I should add, with a note of sadness, that this didn't work out quite as Biblically as he had hoped because his wife subsequently died anyway (not of COVID). I should express sympathy, as that is the conventional thing to do, but actually I have no sympathy to give because it was all used up on the people who ended their life during lockdown because they didn't see the point in living any more.

Not content with killing people by imprisoning them in their own home, the leader of Wales has come for fun wherever he sees it.

Driving is a freedom he simply refuses to tolerate. In Wales the speed limit on many of the motorways is 50mph – for the purposes of air quality, you understand. And it's 20mph anywhere that has more than one house and a pavement – what passes in Wales for a built-up area.

I don't know if you have ever tried to drive 50mph on a motorway. Or 20mph anywhere else. But it is close to impossible.

You spend more time looking at your speedometer than the road, and even when you are driving, the constant sense that you are being controlled by some external force triggers your mind to flick V signs into thin air. I hate it.

More than that, I hate the thought that it's being forced on people. I remember the first few months after passing my driving test – flying about country lanes, whizzing about independently, imagining journeys I would take. Never a concern about speed restrictions or cameras, because there rarely were any.

The only time I was caught doing 54 in a 30mph zone showing off to my fella, I was able to ring the camera people and have a little chat, and they let me off – for reasons I am unclear about. But that was the world we lived in back then.

Now, the sense of being watched dominates any curiosity about where you are trying to go or having fun.

The ridiculously slow speed means you can have a conversation with the person in the car next to you as you go down the motorway. On my recent trip to Swansea me and the bloke driving alongside me exchanged exasperated gestures and then took it in turn to do wanking signs.

My hand gestures were absolutely aimed at Mark Drakeford although, come to think of it, the guy in the car next to me may just have thought I was offering to wank him off and was confirming how long he wanted me to do that for and how much he was prepared to pay.

The thought I have been advertising hand-job services on the motorway in Wales is a bit disturbing. No matter.

It doesn't end in Wales. It's worse for the kids.

My daughters Indy and Poppy have both passed their driving test. I will add that they did this on their own without any funding from me. And they have both bought cars, and taxed and insured them themselves too. They do this old-fashioned thing called work. I know, I know, not many teenagers are into it, but mine always knew if they wanted something they were going to need to pay for it.

I feel deeply sorry for any teenager who wants to perform the simple act of driving from 2023 onwards. They are being crucified.

For starters, they are brainwashed at schools and colleges that cars are deeply evil, and responsible for the destruction of penguins on ice floes somewhere distant that they will probably never visit. The very idea of driving anything other than a toy car with a battery should be abhorrent to them. And if they do dare to drive something their mum or dad would call a 'proper car', they will be penalised through the tax and insurance system until they can't afford the bloody thing anyway.

Driving lessons are almost impossible to come by. If you can find some maniac earning £50 an hour for sitting on his or her arse demonstrating the basic function of driving a car, there is a waitlist to secure their tutelage. The instructor knows they have the upper hand in the marketplace so can act like an asshole and get away with it. Poppy's instructor was one hour late for a lesson – without any warning or apology.

And if that doesn't have your teen crying with frustration on their bedroom floor, out of cash, patience and will – then try getting a driving test.

Back in my day lessons and tests were something you booked the day before or whenever you felt brave enough. Nowadays it's like frigging meat lines in Cuba, queuing forever to try and secure a test slot. If you hit the jackpot and score a driving exam six months in the future, the test sits there like a menacing frog in the road every time you get in a car.

You may not be quite ready yet, you may not be able to afford the lessons you need in time, you may have some kind of life drama that makes it the worst time in your life to be doing a test.

But you feel trapped into doing it because the thought of having to cancel it, lose your money and wait another full six months for another slot is too awful to think about.

How the hell is all this a 17-year-old kid's problem, when all they want to do is drive a bloody car?

And without warning, insurance policies are pulled, or removed, or you are told they are not going to be renewed. No reason or rationale given. No one would ever actually dare claim on their insurance policy because they would never get another one. So it's essentially just another form of taxation.

In my daughter Poppy's case, she was told her provider was no longer going to be in the market, so she is on her own. She searched about for a new provider and the only thing she could find cost £4,500 a year. It was the same story for her 18-year-old friends. It's a scandal – yet no one is yelling about it because young people are supposed to all live in a city and be thrilled about being on a bus or scooter or something.

If you happen to be a farmer living in the middle of nowhere and have a licence to drive tractors, handlers and trucks – you are penalised to death for trying to be a functioning member of society.

If there is one element of this that makes me want to go and punch a green nazi square in the face, it's the 'black box'. You may be blissfully unaware about these. You may even think I am exaggerating for effect. Please go check with a young person you trust (who is not a greenie retard).

Even after earning their own money to pay for their lessons, and their car, and their insurance, and their tax, and their petrol, our kids are still not free. In order to afford even basic insurance they have to agree to be spied on. More still, they have to agree to have their hard-earned freedom to drive restricted and limited.

These insurance firms send out spyware connected to mobile phones, and the spyware has to be placed in the car. If you haven't seen the device, it's typically a little black box or sticky circle.

In order to bring down the cost of the insurance, the kids then have to impose limits on themselves to restrict how they use the car – for example, only driving so many miles from home, not driving after 6pm at night, not taking any passengers with them, never going over the speed limit, not braking too hard or going too fast round corners, not driving in the dark. The list goes on and on. Truly, even trying to tell you about it, I find my teeth clenched and my shoulders pinched, such is the rage I feel. The smallness of little people, getting high on crushing ordinary people's freedom to drive! And more importantly, curtailing young people's freedom to have fun.

I am not exaggerating. I am not being typical me, over-dramatising for fun and effect. I truly believe that the freedom to drive is a real moment for a young person – where all of a sudden you are in a car and your brain realizes, 'I could go anywhere!'

The naughtiness this enables, the endless choices it presents, are like an explosion in your head. At least, that's how it was for me. I drove like a maniac around country lanes. I was loaned my dad's massive family car to rock up to work in, a little girl in a massive man-sized car. I even understood, taking one particularly hairy corner that did not look like it was going to end well for me, that I now had the freedom to kill myself in a multitude of ways without my parents being able to save me.

These are massive realisations. And I say all that as a girl.

Now I have a son who is a car obsessive. Already a Saturday boy at the local garage, he can complete a car service on his own at 15, and I see a whole other dimension. I believe that for boys, car ownership is a key transition to manhood. For girls, if a boy has a car it's a sign that he's going places. Not in a financial way, just as an indication that he offers more fun and freedom because he can get to places without help or a parent's permission.

Lovely Mark smashed his way through four cars before he decided he might need to start driving with a bit more care. There's nothing big or clever about this and we can all be wise and say that life is short or what a waste it would have been had he been hurt. But it's a rite of passage Mark doesn't regret, and one my son is keen to begin.

All this 'smalling' of our lives is deliberate, of course. We'll talk more about that in a minute.

If you aren't aware of what's going on, you might just think it's a tough time to be a teenager and drive. You might just look at insurance premiums and think they are crazy. Or try to come up with a rational explanation why it's impossible to secure driving lessons or a test. Parents will always swoop in to cover the costs and try to take some of the burden off their young. And things will keep going down the trajectory they are headed on.

But if you have your eyes open, even just a little bit, you'll understand there's a deliberate and coordinated effort to take away our right to drive in the UK. In 2022 I predicted, publicly, that within five years we would no longer have the right to drive a private car – that would be by 2027.

What better way to achieve this than to cut off the supply of people able to drive? If you deter and prevent young people learning, the banning of private cars will have no impact on them and these docile idiots will accept it all as part of 'saving the planet'.

They will never know the rich excitement of sitting in a car on your own for the first time, turning the key and suddenly realising you are free. They will never feel the thrill of doing something you are definitely not supposed to be doing in a car that is not your own, or feel the incredible power of escape to be found by getting in a car and just driving because that's the only thing that makes sense.

I think about the time I just couldn't take it anymore, when my husband had left me, I was home with two babies under 18 months, and I just couldn't pretend for another minute that I was okay. I put those babies into their car seats, drove to my mum and dad's (I'm not sure how I made it) and fell out onto the driveway in a pool of self-pitying tears. They took it from there.

I remember the car, I remember the handbrake (weirdly), I remember my mum's face as she looked at me. And I remember pulling up on their drive.

That's what a car is for: a means of getting away, of going somewhere to get help, if not for your sake then for the sake of the little people who deserve better than the broken heap of you.

It's not just the right to drive that's under threat. It's all this glorious freedom that the tyrants who govern us are plotting to take away.

21 July

In what I suspect will become a fast family tradition, we have made the frankly ostentatious decision to rent a villa in Corfu for a couple of weeks for the Team Hopkins / Cross family vacation.

(Here in the UK we typically use the word holiday but I prefer the American term vacation. It sounds more exotic and I need all the exotic I can get.)

In my home I am the ideas woman, and having come up with the idea of a family vacation in a villa on the Med, in order to try and bring together all our children now working different jobs in different places, I made the error of allowing Lovely Mark to book the place.

Lovely Mark, as we know, has elevated tastes, despite being married to me and coming from the wrong side of Watford. A few grand later, a perfect, gleaming white palace was ours for ten days, perched atop a hill in an idyllic little fishing bay two across from the fancy-pants bay where luxury, mega-massive super-yachts are moored.

He was very proud of himself, as if he had just hunted down a very hard-to-find bargain at a cut-price store.

But who am I to argue? You will know I am not flash, we are not flash. There are times of being able to earn good money, and times when we were forced to sell the family home. My resulting view on all of this is that if there are moments of gloriousness, best make the most of them. And so the 'family trip to luxury villa' was born.

Lovely Mark used to come here back in the day with of a former life. I object to this massively because, despite being the harridan that stole Mark away, I demand that he pretend I am the only woman in his world and he has never slept with or kissed anyone else ever.

However, Mark has stories here, and if he has stories it means there existed a time when I wasn't in his life – which CLEARLY cannot be the case.

Either way, I love it. I love the sun. I love the fact it is scorchioooo from morning till night and I love the cat that thinks it his divine right to live inside our perfect villa and who stands at the fridge complaining until you give him the chicken or milk to which he considers himself entitled.

Poppy had an unfortunate incident on day two, falling asleep face-down in the sun with zero suntan lotion and waking up with a bright red arse and matching shoulders. You might argue it is my job as a mother to help protect her against such things, but having funded the holiday, collected her from the airport, bought her an excellent white linen jumpsuit, and provided food and drinks for the duration, plus an ample supply of suntan lotion on the kitchen table, you will forgive me if I assumed she might do this one thing for herself.

Am I supposed to apply suntan lotion to her arse at 18?

This is the thing with mothering. Once you are a mum you are always a mum. And no matter how hard you work, or how much you provide, or any amount of lovely things you try and do for your children, it will never be quite enough. You will never escape that feeling that if you had only…

If I had just taken the suntan lotion off the kitchen table for her and rubbed it on her arse, she wouldn't have got burned.

Some things kids just have to learn for themselves and at some point mothers just have to know that, even if it involves some discomfort on the part of your lovely kiddies. They might, in the process, learn something necessary for them to go on to do the right thing in future.

Lovely Mark has the same view about rent. My heart says it's a horrible thing to charge your own children rent because they need a place to live. The world is dreadfully expensive and I want them to know this is always their home and they will always find help here.

Lovely Mark says kids need to learn to pay rent otherwise how will they ever learn, why would they ever leave, and when he was a boy he had to hand over much of what he earned to his mum and dad. I think that is really bloody tough and suspect Lovely Mark was treated rather harshly by his father at times.

So we came to a kind of compromise position where my oldest pays a kind of notional rent to Lovely Mark... And then I privately let her know that he is actually putting this in a savings account so that one day she will be able to use it for a deposit. I suspect all parties involved know all the above, but we each keep our understanding quiet because everyone seems to be happy. Functioning dysfunctionalism – that's my family motto and I am sticking with it.

You will know if you are a long-time follower, that I have always tried to protect my family from my noise and have maintained a pretty strong wall between them and my 'public' life. I never post anything about any of them on social media, nor share our private family plans or anything from our life, as many do with their holidays and good times.

But in the relative privacy of this book, I can quietly confide that we had the most lovely holiday together and I spent a lot of time in Corfu feeling hugely grateful that we had kind of made it through, together.

I know there is more to come. I know there will be disasters. I know I will be the cause of many of them.

But I am grateful to my family for sticking with me. I am incredibly thankful that my children are alive, happy and working hard. And most of all I am thrilled that we all chose to be together for those ten days in the Med.

Though I will add, when Lovely Mark books the villa the kids know they are on to a good thing. And frankly if you don't want to come on a fully funded family holiday to a lovely villa and get taken out for drinks and dinner, you really are a proper moron.

AUGUST

Did you know that since 1949 the FBI has kept its top-ten most-wanted list meticulously updated and available for all to see?

Ten Most Wanted Fugitives

Notice: The official FBI Ten Most Wanted Fugitives list is maintained on the FBI website. This information may be copied and distributed, however, any unauthorised alteration of any portion of the FBI's Ten Most Wanted Fugitives posters is a violation of federal law (18 U.S.C., Section 709). Persons who make or reproduce these alterations are subject to prosecution and, if convicted, shall be fined or imprisoned for not more than one year, or both.

I am guessing they are trying to say that if you recreate the list and cut and paste one of your relatives onto it, you are in big trouble and will find yourself doing time. So, take a breath before you go right ahead and stitch up a family member (as I was just about to do).

If you take a moment to look at the ten most-wanted,

you can usually see why. At least three of this latest haul look like they would steal from their grandma even after she was dead. And one must surely have some kind of machete-based murder to his name.

My particular favourite is this guy: Vitel'Homme Innocent.

There is a $2 million reward out for this dude. As leader of the gang 'Kraze Barye', he allegedly did a spot of kidnapping of Christian missionaries, holding them at gunpoint for 17 days and possibly killing a few others.

Not to minimise the horror suffered by the alleged victims, but there are a couple of points that stand out.

Firstly, his mother had the wisdom to name him Innocent, or more specifically 'Quick The Innocent Man', which is a direct translation of his Haitian French name, which he is clearly living up to: despite having a $2 million bounty on his head, he has been so quick the FBI has yet to track him down.

I have no wish to besmirch the reputation of the many good Haitians I know, but it is not realistic to imagine no one on the island would have dobbed him in by now in exchange for being a millionaire twice over.

I very much enjoy the idea that his mother, looking at her new baby in his basket, or wherever Haitians put their babies (in a conch shell?), and seeing the face that we now see wildly gurning out from his FBI mugshot, decided, 'I will name you Innocent.' Clearly she was keenly aware, as only a mother can be, that this crazy-eyed child of hers looked as guilty as sin right from the get-go.

Even in a line-up called Ten Most Wanted Fugitives, it has to be said that Innocent stands out as being someone fairly high on an addictive substance and quite capable of eating your tongue straight out of your face without blinking twice. I am not sure if he invented the name of his gang, Kraze Barye (translated as Destroy the Barrier), but I rather like it. Mostly because in my tiny brain I can imagine our man Innocent with a nickname like Crazy Barry, hanging around the amusements trying to shove his penis in the penny slots.

All of this is to say (she adds casually, 500 words later), that I was wondering about my ten most-wanted. I am not the FBI. And I am not talking about actual criminals (though some are debatable). But given it's August and in the summer holidays we are allowed to do what we want, I thought I might write down my shit-list for your entertainment.

These are my most-wanted fugitives. It should be made clear that none of them are engaged in any criminal activities that I am aware of, and none of them are fugitives. Nor are they actually wanted by me. On the contrary, I'd like all of them to be kept as far away from me as possible. While it is frowned on to wish ill to others, I'd like all these characters to face their comeuppance, mostly for being complete C U Next Tuesdays in real life.

So here you have it. The KH most-wanted fugitives currently hiding on your screens or, more likely, behind highly lucrative consultancy positions, the better to lord over your demise.

1   Davos

I am not directing my ire at the whole of Davos, the highest mountain town in Europe nestled in the snowy hills of Switzerland. You may take everything that skis or snowboards or earns an honest living through snow-based endeavours and place them to one side in the manner of a hyper-sexualised Nigella Lawson cooking show featuring plump sausages in sheer pastry.

It's the rest of the fuckers I abhor. Every stinking one of them.

Founded on 24 January 1971 by German engineer Klaus Schwab, the World Economic Forum and everyone associated with it represents everything I cannot stand. It's like a concentrate of the stuff that runs through the veins of the ultra-old-money wealthy, the lefty cyclists of Kensington and fancy London, the politicians accruing wealth though powerful connections. A bit of Davos or at least Davos mentality runs through all of them.

The overarching principle is that a small group of exceptionally intelligent individuals is far better placed to secure the future of civilisation than civilisation itself.

These elites are confident that only their kind need protecting and preserving (in bunkers, cryogenic tanks or through extreme medical interventions) and everyone else is a useless meat-eater and completely redundant.

The notion is that civilisation needed people during the agrarian, agricultural and industrial revolutions because labour was vital to keep humans alive, but now we have AI, and non-humans (or part humans) can take things from here. Which would make eight billion humans surplus to requirement.

It's a strange thing. When anyone says eight billion humans everyone kind of nods along, like, okay, we have eight billion humans too many, gotcha.

But when you think about this number at the level of the individual, each with their love of crochet, or the family, or sharing a lovely meal – or when you picture a team of jolly souls trying their best to win at pub-quiz night – then you start to see the horror of that term 'redundant'.

Based on pure functionality, the Davos elite view our family as expendable and useless consumers who need to be controlled, contained and ultimately neutralised.

We are on the path towards our own demise, and control and containment are already playing a role in our lives.

Here are my written predictions for the next five years in black and white. I will be delighted if we can return to these in the future and say that I was wrong:

1   We will not be permitted to own or drive a car.
2   We will not be permitted to travel freely, fly or eat meat.
3   There will be no such thing as cash.
4   We will not be permitted to own our own homes.
5   There will be cull events designed to wipe out large numbers of useless meat-eaters in the numbers required to ultimately achieve a non-human future.

The thing that really grips me about all this (acknowledging that removing the freedoms from eight million people and then euthanising them is actually the real issue here) is the stinking hypocrisy of these monsters plotting our imminent demise.

As they plan to remove our freedom to drive, they take their chauffeured limousines up to Davos and every other meeting and jolly they attend, as do all their family members and associates. Look at Sadiq Khan here in the UK with three SUVs in cavalcade to take him four miles from home to walk his dog.

While we lose the will to even attempt flying anywhere thanks to costs, delays and other endless nonsense, these massive assholes fly in and out on their private jets between their many meetings and their many homes on many different continents.

While we are forcibly regulated and regimented, they plan for a world where they will be completely free – free even from the need to pretend they are working in the best interests of humanity. As their plan gathers momentum, all the niceties will be dispensed with.

Forced into state-controlled accommodation, expected to live only in the metaverse, unable to travel, gather or eat as we please, we will wonder how all of this could have happened without anyone stopping it.

Unless of course we stop it right now. And here's my other prediction: the fight back is on. We rise up and refuse to be controlled. And we take numbers 1 to 5 above and we shove them up Klaus Schwab's arse, sideways. Death is too good for that monster.

2   Fauci

For the avoidance of doubt about my personal views, I believe Fauci had a hand in creating the first pandemic and engineering its release from a lab at Chinese New Year. I believe this was his five-to-ten-year mission set for him by the Davos overlords, and he triumphed at it.

I believe the pandemic (Covid / Plandemic, etc) was a controlled experiment to better understand how to control and limit eight billion people with a view to a future cull event.

I am perfectly happy to have you disagree with me, think I am bonkers or not believe a word I am saying. Both things – my thoughts and yours – can run in parallel without us ever needing to fall out or hide from each other.

I believe evil does walk this earth and sometimes we come into contact with it. Even at low levels our sensors detect it: that spider sense you get that something about a person isn't quite right. I have met powerful men and have felt every inch of my neck spasm with the certainty I am in the presence of real darkness.

I see Fauci with a tail and scales. I see his slime trail as he puppets his part in all of this. And I would happily end him, in the certain belief I had done my part to help save ordinary people.

His British counterpart, Chris Whitty, is embedded in this circle of malevolence, as is every government-attached representative of the Science that was brought in, on orders from WEF, to brainwash the people because we were brought up to respect the Science and if the Science is talking, and especially if it wears a white coat over its scales, we shut up and listen.

The pandemic handbook exists. Each nation followed the same handbook, with regional variations for credibility, and each nation had specific WEF enforcers to ensure maximum fear as the mechanism of control.

For this reason, I, along with a great many others, will never trust medicine or those who push it ever again.

3 China

I appreciate there are many good Chinese out there. And, hand on heart, as New York City was shuttered down around me at 8pm on 23 March 2020 while I waited to do a speech – also cancelled – my last act was to go out and buy a Chinese meal. My heart broke for all those small businesses the government was sending to the wall.

It is racist to be against a people simply on the basis of their colour or their differences. However, this isn't a race thing – it's the sense that evil moves quickly in China. The idea that one man has the ability to completely control 1.4 billion people has to be inspiring to the evil that calls Davos its political home.

4 Brendan Cox (ex-Save the Children)

Even if someone knew all there is to know about Brendan Cox – the ex-Save the Children twat – they would keep their mouths shut because he has very powerful friends in very important places. And the kind of access to supportive cash and legal defence that makes things like complaints against him for assault and battery of a woman completely disappear.

He is one of those powerful men who set off just about every trigger I have in my body warning me that darkness is at my doorstep.

There's plenty against him that is documented. Like the claims of sexual harassment and inappropriate behaviour by Mr Cox while at Save the Children. Save the Children UK faced accusations for several years that it failed to properly investigate both him and his boss.

Or the claims in the Mail on Sunday that he had assaulted a woman in her 30s at Harvard University in 2015. Police filed her complaint as assault and battery but action against him was dropped. Cox denied these claims but admitted making mistakes in a previous role with the charity Save the Children.

If you recall, the murder of Jo Cox, just before the Brexit vote, was seen as the kind of societal trigger that could ensure a Remain win (coincidence, I am sure).

To quote the Guardian: 'Brendan's wife, Jo Cox, a Labour MP, was attacked outside her constituency office in West Yorkshire by a "rightwing terrorist" during the EU referendum campaign in June 2016.'

So then he set up the More in Common charity and the Jo Cox Foundation, mere moments after his wife was brutally murdered, apparently able to conduct press interviews and write media columns when most of us would be lying on the floor with our kids wondering how we would continue to breathe.

Just so you have the full story, Cox resigned from his posts at More in Common and the Jo Cox Foundation after being publicly accused of sexual assault.

And honestly, nothing could surprise me less in this sorry tale of darkness than to learn that Cox is now remarried to a violence against women campaigner, Anna Ryder.

To be absolutely clear, just in case you are confused about his new wife's choice of husband, given Cox's track record of alleged battery, assault and sexual impropriety, Miss Ryder doesn't campaign for violence against women, but against violence against women. She works for a group that supports the bereaved families of victims of violence.

Cox happily trotted onto ITV's Lorraine show to brag about his new wife: 'We are both very much looking forward to celebrating with our families.'

He said he and Jo had previously discussed the idea of remarrying if either of them died. The father of two told Lorraine that Jo had said she would want him to remarry.

I swear his level of darkness knows no limits. How does a man with multiple accusations of sexual assault behind him, resignations here and there to avoid scrutiny, and a face that could freeze the tits on a poker bear – end up on the sofa at ITV to chat about his new wife, a campaigner against violence against women? Like, how is that a thing?

And how does this cretin get to sit there and speak for his murdered wife?

'I always knew that she would want that,' he said. 'But I never thought it would happen because when you lose someone like Jo, you never think you'll find somebody with the energy and the love and the enthusiasm and the excitement that Jo had. I'm incredibly lucky that I have.'

He added that his children were 'very excited' when he told them that he intended to propose to Ryder. 'I said: "I'm thinking about asking her to marry me. What do you think?" I think their response was, "You're never going to do any better than Anna," which I think was basically a nice thing and a compliment,' he said. 'They're very excited about it.'

I'm not certain it was a compliment. 'You're never going to do any better than Anna' is not the reassurance I'd be looking for from my kids, to be fair. I'd consider that line pretty harsh.

But here's the thing: it's not even all this stuff that has put him here on my most-wanted list. It's something far darker.

On the day that the Matrix came for me and pulled on the net they had fully encircled me with, Brendan Cox's name was right there with those others who came to annihilate me from the face of the planet. The Chief Rabbi's Office, the Board of Deputies, the Muslim Council, the Labour Party and the Conservative party goons – all of them had letters with multiple signatories ready to lodge with my editor to have me annulled from life. And that's before we start on the media barons, Murdoch, Paul Dacre et al.

I have stood on the shores of southern Italy watching the Save the Children ferry boat preparing to head out into the Med to rendezvous with the illegal people-traffickers sending flesh from Libya. I have spoken to the crew, phoned the Save the Children HQ to try to be allowed on board, and tracked the ship's movements with the assistance of shipping specialists.

And I spent time sitting with its inevitable cargo of human flesh dumped on the shoreline to be processed by those coining it in from this trade in humans. Women from these boats and others, now prostitutes run by pimps, paying back the debt they owed for their place on board.

The Matrix is funded by this trade in human flesh, I am sure of it. And I am certain it involves heads of churches, synagogues and mosques. I believe it involves heads of political parties, of charities and banking, and landed money that is preserved through the generations.

As one exhausted immigration official told me, all roads lead to Rome. I hold some of the evidence that proves it.

It is my personal opinion that Mr Cox is a deeply evil thing walking among us. My opinion is only compounded by his bizarre redemption. All the damage, all the harm, all the hurt he is alleged to have caused never touches him. Worse still, he is invited to gurn on the couch of daytime TV, to be approved and lauded by the establishment of which he is part.

Others out there know much more and still hold their tongue. Perhaps they still have things to lose? I am lucky. In taking all that I had, this same Matrix also set me free.

5 The Billy Big Bollocks Self-Preserving For One More Day

I know we are supposed to be talking about individuals here, and so far we've had a host of Davos bastards and the Chinese – if we were trying to make a poster, we would struggle. I figure Davos would be represented by Charles Schwaab and the Chinese by Xi Jinping.

Can I just add that I bloody love the correct pronunciation of the leader of China? She Gin Ping! Like, how cool is it to be called She Gin? And why couldn't I have been called that? Obviously I'm less obsessed with the Ping bit. I'd want 'drinks', or 'crazy-cow' as my third bit: She Gin Crazy-Cow. But I would like the Chinese leader to know that She Gin Ping rocks. And he should consider adding Pong to his name just for Western giggles: She Gin Ping-Pong.

Perhaps you are starting to understand my brain a little and why it is so incredibly difficult to stick to a task. And why sometimes I need to vacuum the floors just to fill my front brain with stuff so mundane the rest of me gets a rest. It is exhausting up there, as many of you who share my kind of massively-on-the-spectrum brain will understand.

Back to my next fugitive, and once again it is an umbrella gathering of people of the same type. But if we were to give it a face, I'd choose Andrew Lawrence.

I know, I hear you. Who TF is Andrew Lawrence? Never heard of the fella.

Right. You have never heard of him and that's no

problem. I love it when people say they have no clue who I am. In fact, those are by far my favourite kind of people, as we are both meeting each other for the first time and I am pretty all right in the flesh.

But Andrew Lawrence believes he and his little bunch of fanboys are very big news indeed. Which is okay, because it takes a certain amount of ego to do anything in public, let alone try and be funny.

Andrew Lawrence is a small-club stand-up who organises Comedy Unleashed, a gathering of Conservative or cancelled comedians and brings them to venues so that ordinary people can have a laugh at the madness. I understand he also has a slot on GB News. Please understand that I one-hundred-percent support this and think it is absolutely one of the most important things we should be doing right now.

So much so that even when a number of their comedians have not been that great, or their audience write to me asking me to join the line-up, I am super-happy to help. After all, if you've heard Andrew Williams once, you've heard him every time (same set, different venue).

So at the request of the Comedy Unleashed audience, I have been in touch with Andrew to offer to join them. I have offered to be their warm-up, to help sell tickets when they are struggling, or to fill slots for those who are just repeating an old set.

But he doesn't respond, at least not to me.

He did tell the lovely supporter who was campaigning for me to be included that they were not keen on having me because:

a   they didn't find me funny and
b   they weren't keen on the sort of audience I would
    bring.

I can add a c) to that.

And here's where this whole Billy Big Bollocks Self-Preserving For One More Day comes in.

These are the boys who coast along on the rebellion side of life. They are on 'our side', they are all pro 'free speech', they are 'fighting back against the madness', they are 'free thinkers'. But the other common denominator is that they all still have paid jobs and bosses to please. They are all able to attract other lucrative engagements or at least the odd side hustle.

Because they have paid jobs – Spectator, GB News, Spiked, Free Speech Union or whatever – they are in this peculiar space where they are reliant on the 'free speech' audience, but are still absolutely willing to throw those on the front lines under a bus, or to censor them if it means they can self-preserve for one more day.

GB News is a great example. It is the closest thing to a regular British news channel that we have. But if you are on payroll you have to agree to censor those on the naughty list: Tommy Robinson, Laurence Fox, myself... The list goes on.

This willingness to censor applies to Neil Oliver, Brendan O'Neill, Andrew Lawrence, Toby Young and all the rest. All of them are perfectly willing to act like

Tommy, myself, Laurence, Mark Steyn and others, but they act like we don't even exist in order to avoid catching the 'cancelled' bug. They are scared that by association, they too will be cancelled. That if they work alongside any of us from the gutter, they will be dragged down there too.

I think this little band of controlled boys would all say that:

· This all sounds like sour grapes, that I am just jealous they are still in employment when I lost all of my jobs.
· If I shut up and did what I was told a bit more I would still have jobs.
· It is better to have a voice to speak out with than for us all to be cancelled.
· We must not attack our own side. Any time we are shooting inside the tent we are losing.

And I agree wholeheartedly with all of these statements. They are absolutely correct. This is why in the real world (which doesn't include this book I am writing which, clearly, doesn't exist and therefore I am able to spill my heart and soul into it, and show my underwear without self-censorship – right up to the day it comes back from the printers and I look at 3,000 copies and realise people are going to read this and see me and I will be naked in front of you all... Oh Lordy Lord), in the real world I hold my tongue and outwardly support all these boys and repeat the mantra that voices on platforms are better than silence in exile.

Happily, the number of good souls in exile is growing

apace and I am delighted to find myself among strong men and women who have been willing to pay the ultimate price for sticking to their personal beliefs: Russell Brand, doctors and nurses who spoke out against the vaccine, Laurence Fox, Tommy, the Jan 6'ers, MAGA Americans, farmers, truckers, builders, military men and others.

When it comes to picking a side, there is not a day that I doubt which is the one to be on. And as much as the lesser boys try to self-preserve, I also know we will be here for them if they man up or find themselves ejected for crossing whichever new line they are obliged to tiptoe around.

You can only toe the line for so long. Eventually the line becomes so fine that even with your girly feet, you find yourself on the wrong side of it.

There is another point here and it is one Americans make very well. We are stronger together. Look at the NHS 100k shining like a beacon on a hill. Because the NHS 100k stuck together in their refusal to be forcibly injected with mRNA at the behest of the government, because the majority refused to fold and because they were so many in number, the government was forced to back down.

It wasn't easy for any of them. Most had already had their final interview before termination, some lost marriages and homes as a result, some were forced out by their own families for non-compliance, most were devastated by the knowledge they would lose the career they loved – all that on top of the sheer brutality of former work mates and 'friends'.

Yet they stood together.

Meanwhile I ran up and down this fine country with nothing to offer but cuddles and praise for them all, and it's a message I continue to shout onstage. These brave women and men are an inspiration and I salute them. They are the example.

Imagine the GB News bosses if the whole presenting team said they would stop presenting when Mark Steyn was effectively forced out for speaking against the vaccine-injured and grooming gangs. He received a bunch of Ofcom warnings and complaints and was then handed a new contract stipulating he would have to pay his own Ofcom fines – a ridiculous contract he was quite right not to sign.

The 'free speech' boys simply turned their backs to self-preserve for one more day.

Neil Oliver chose self-preservation and his pay packet over standing up for Mark Steyn, for all his dramatic monologues to camera about speaking truth, which his supporters like to retweet. I see the self-preservation in him and it repulses me.

It is a dilemma. What's better: some voices or no voices?

But could it be resolved if the remaining voices held the line? Surely if all the GB News presenters had refused to present until Steyn had a workable contract, a contract would have been found?

Self-preservation is just cowardice, and another mechanism of control (refer to all of Jewish history for details). I lay this charge at the door of Brendan O'Neill and his 'free speech' cos play. And Toby Young. And Neil Oliver. And Andrew Lawrence. And Farage to some extent (except he is deadly effective and we need him), and the rest. You know who you are.

Life is good here in the home of authentic free speakers. I wouldn't switch it up for a moment. I just encourage others to stop treating the cancelled like an inconvenient plague that can be ignored.

6 Jeremy Vine

Jeremy Vine is as irritating as thrush and equally as hard to get rid of. But my question is how someone so universally loathed by ordinary Brits can still be plastered all over the BBC and other channels? His name elicits howls of dismay from my audiences because they can't stand him. They know something is off with this one.

He even caused the hashtag #BikeNonce to trend for three days straight on X. That's quite the achievement.

I hold him personally responsible for the length of sentencing received by my friend Alex Belfield, convicted for online stalking in 2022. Turning on the tears in court, saying he was frightened for his daughters, and pushing the phrase 'the Jimmy Saville of Stalking' as a pre-prepared headline for the papers, was all part of getting Belfield sentenced under a brand-new law, made up just for him, with special new sentencing guidelines that mean he will serve far longer in jail than a rapist, murderer or paedophile.

For any number of reasons, Jeremy Vine is on my most-wanted list. Sometimes I sit back and smile because I know with certainty that if you wait by the river long enough, the bodies of your enemies will come floating by. Having seen Schofield float past already, it can only be a matter of time.

7   Nadal

It's a little bit harsh that Nadal is one of the few individual faces in this line-up, but he is a particularly foul example of a whole raft of people whose attitude to mandatory vaccination stunk harder than a skunk on blue cheese.

I always thought he was a hotty-botty back in the day when he had a full head of Spanish hair, a well-oiled tan and a chest to die for. I could quite imagine myself snuggled up against it as he sipped Robinsons lemon squash under the sun-shade at Wimbledon.

But those days are long gone, for two reasons.

The first is pure sexual objectification, of which I am quite proud. Nadal the hot Spanish conquistador has been replaced by an ageing and balding European with an angry demeanour and more nervous tics than a Tourettes chick on Prozac. You know how much I love a weirdo, but it has to be said that if you are a tennis player in tight white shorts, having a tic that requires you to touch your nuts and drag your knickers out your arse 15 times before you can even begin to play ball – well, it's not a good look.

And as for balding, no one can help that. But you can

help trying to hold on to the last few hairs that used to make up your hair line, imagining that people won't notice. Andre Agassi had the right approach (and a beautiful head, I might add). Unless you have a head that is now shaped like mine post cranial surgery, then I suggest you get the shaver out and man the fuck up.

However, none of this is actually the point. The point is, Nadal was one of the many unforgivables who not only sucked up the vaccine but also applauded the exclusion of Djokovic from the Australian Open because of his refusal to be forcibly injected.

Nadal was asked if he felt sorry for Djokovic, given he was first held at the airport, then sent to quarantine, then threatened with forcible deportation. The Spaniard's response indicated that his sympathy was limited; Nadal said that decisions come with consequences, as was the case for Djokovic after his decision to fly to Melbourne despite being unvaccinated.

'I think if he wanted, he would be playing here in Australia without a problem. He made his own decisions, and everybody is free to take their own decisions, but then there are some consequences. Of course I don't like the situation that is happening. In some way I feel sorry for him. But at the same time he knew the conditions since a lot of months ago, so he makes his own decision.'

Sports people at his level spend their whole lives obsessing about what they do to their bodies, and what they put into them. And yet many swallowed the idea they needed the state injectable like it made all the sense in the world.

You are one of the fittest men on the entire planet and yet you still think you need something manmade in a lab to be injected into you? I mean, please.

Instead of actually supporting Djokovic and saying, unless he plays I'm not playing either, he reinforced the crazy Australian government's position. Again, if just a handful of the top players – even just the top four – had stuck together, Djokovic would have been allowed to play. But they happily threw him under the bus.

There are many like Nadal, who went in hard from their position of influence to say that the unvaccinated should be locked up, or kept in their homes, or denied medical treatment – Piers Morgan, Esther Rantzen and Andrew Neil, just for a start.

Many have since tried to squirm away from what they said. But their words should be permanently linked to their names; it's important to remember who we are dealing with in the future. And which of these individuals has the courage to think for him or herself.

8   Sister Bede

My mother says you shouldn't speak ill of the dead. But then again, my mother says a lot of things that are best ignored.

Plus there are a lot of dead people who were complete arseholes in life and I don't see why they should get a free pass just because they laid down for the long sleep and never got up again.

I know I can be a right pain in the arse, but at school – particularly at the age of 8 – I wasn't. Not wishing to toot my own horn, but I found everything way too easy: schoolwork, homework, sport, music, whatever – I got it done quick-fast and was top of the class.

That was until I entered the classroom of Sister Bede, an Irish nun in full habit and veil who decided it was her mission in life to bring me down a peg or ten. And she really went for it.

Sister Bede is the reason I have no trouble at all believing nuns capable of offering refuge to girls pregnant outside marriage and killing off the babies through mistreatment. Sister Bede could have done that without blinking.

I want her to know, even in death, that I have not forgotten. I have not forgotten my left hand being tied behind my back because it was unGodly to be left-handed. I have not forgotten being kept in every lunchtime to learn to write with my right. I have not forgotten the downgrading, the unkindness and the miserable feeling of knowing something was right and being marked wrong.

I may have been a lucky kid who found life too easy, but I was not your ball to kick around. And I only wish I had found this big voice 40 years earlier so I could have told you to your face that what you were doing was wrong, and that certain Irish nuns are some of the cruellest beasts ever to roam this planet.

The moral of the story is that abstinence makes you angry. Have more sex. Do not become Sister Bede.

9   YouTuber Josh Pieters

He's the chap that pretended to be a South African farmer under attack, flew me to Prague, stalked me in the street, secretly filmed me at my hotel, paid a room full of actors to pretend to be anxious South African farming families, and then put a CUNT sign up behind me after I made a short speech expressing my commitment to the South Africans that I love.

He's not here on this list because he made me look like a fool in front of 25 million people (although he did).

He's here on the list because he used something I love and care about in order to achieve it. I went with kindness and came back with a good hard punch in the face.

10 David Cameron

Remember that thing we said about how you can feel the evil in some people? This guy is darkness walking.

SEPTEMBER

3 September

It completely blows my mind.

At what point did we lose the ability to use a phone like a phone, for private communications, and start using video instead, whacking the sound up loud so we can shout our conversation at our daughter / husband / kid / girlfriend /mate as if everyone else on the damn train wants to listen in – both to us and whoever we're talking to, who has no idea that half the carriage on the Taunton to Paddington line is being forced to listen to them shout their conversation at each other.

I get the bit about not always wanting the phone so close to your head, now that we know that everything is at all times trying to give us cancer – and that's before we get started on 5G antennas and how bad they might be for us. The idea of holding something Apple has a hand in up close to your grey matter is less appealing than it was.

I have observed the evolution of audio into visual – not a single radio show or musical experience is complete without some twat filming it or putting it on screen. Ears started to become redundant in the early 2000s and now they only perform about half the functions that used to be required for them.

I swear the majority of shouty Facetimers love the fact that everyone can hear them shouting away, making a performance of a moment in their lifestory. Like the bit on The X Factor where the contestant tries to make you like them, but a lot more shit.

The woman that pulled this stunt at the bar tonight was filming her grandkids and her daughter, talking baby-talk to the little ones who were unable to get a word in edgeways over Grandma.

'What a lovely dancer you are, you clever girl!' shouted Grandma across the bar.

The bloke next to me shared a friendly raised eyebrow and I took to downing my Merlot to numb the pain.

Heading to the gym, I walked in on a chunky bird who had mounted a spinning bike and was sweating and pedalling in equal measure. The most well-known static bike brand is Peloton, which I suspect will fall into administration before this book even gets to print as people start to realise sitting on a pretend bike in your cold garage being shouted at is not all that fun.

If you aren't aware of how these infernal bikes work, they have a video screen on which you select a workout program to view a pre-filmed trainer leading an exercise class to the accompaniment of blaring dance music.

Typically American, these spin-class instructors are

all built like Caitlyn Jenner (the javelin years), and have teeth whiter than a ginger's arse and the sort of pneumatic boobs that glisten with sweat but never bounce or buckle.

'YOU OWE IT TO YOURSELF!' the silly moo is yelling from the bike's screen as Chunky Girl puffs away wondering if she really does owe this to herself at all.

I fancy that the moment the torture class ends and she dismounts her bicycle, she will decide she owes herself a Big Mac and large fries – and that caramel-crunch shake can't hurt now that she has put in a shift in with Jolene or whatever the pneumatic bird is called.

Some people actually buy these bikes and do the workouts at home. The companies that make them made a mint during COVID when posh people with too much money, concerned about their exercise regimen and not wanting to break any rules or catch anything from the plebeians marauding about the streets with their germs, invested heavily in both the equipment and the gear that comes with it.

By now I imagine most of these machines are festering in spare rooms or garages, being used mainly to hang the ironing on. Or to prop open a door.

Exercise is a funny thing. People much prefer purchasing the kit to doing the work. You can even avoid doing the thing by just purchasing more kit, always the preferable option. See dickheads out for a run wearing more tech than a chuffing Google engineer for details.

Whether it's phone conversations, gym bikes or running, I stand by my assertion that tech has only hindered effort and misguided people's attention from being seen or heard or both.

5 September

Holy crap bags. ITV's This Morning show decided to bring back Holly Willoughbooby. Instead of just acknowledging that the This Morning sofa without Phil would be like Chaz without Dave and walking away with some dignity and quite possibly some sympathy from her adoring fans, old bouncy boobies tried to hang on to her contract like a desperate XL bully clinging to the arm of a small child.

In part, I blame her husband, a very odd, ferreting little man with far too much influence and way too little personality. Their relationship is a very odd one indeed. You look at him and wonder a) how did he end up with so much clout in TV land, and b) how did he end up married to the fairly good-looking Holly Boobs.

I have no answers to these questions, but undoubtedly with his encouragement Holly made the very ill-fated decision to return to This Morning. It's up there with all the worst comebacks in history – like the Steps reunion (which killed off one of their member) or the wife that takes back her cheating husband only to be let down again a few months later.

I am guessing the producers were going for full-fat cheese with an extra sprinkling of Pilgrims Choice, because the relaunch was about as gag-inducing as a soft porn shoot with Big Black Brian and his Mighty Schlong.

Out bowled Holly and Hammond, dancing to 'Having the time of our life', which they clearly were not. The only advantage of having Alison Hammond as a dancing partner is she can make anyone look cute and petite. She could make the Disney Carnival Cruise ship look like a Kinder egg toy. Or perhaps I'm being fat-ist. Or racist. Or both.

Everyone was cringing. I could tell the camera and sound crew were clenching their pelvic floors in horror. Anyone on team that could hide, become invisible or stick their head behind a massive bit of scenery was doing exactly that.

No one believed the charade. Not Holly. Not the audience at home. Not even chumba-wumba Hammond who valiantly does her best to make everything seem okay despite being morbidly obese.

And within four weeks Holly was gone. ITV conveniently dug up a stalker and Holly was suddenly terrified for her life and her family's safety and withdrew from the show.

A poor fat man with mental-health issues was the fall guy, valiantly providing cover so Holly could skulk off – after herself providing cover for a paedophile, going along with his lies when it was convenient, pushing in at the Queen's funeral and then pulling the tearful betrayed act when it all went wrong.

As my mother would say, sometimes all you have to do is wait.

And ding dong, both of them are gone.

10 September

I just reposted my video where I am pretending to be Chris Whitty. Mostly because his name is back in circulation and it's worth reminding good people what a cretin he was in helping force through the lockdown agenda.

But also because there is SO MUCH RAGE everywhere ALL THE TIME that we need a little reminder to stop for a moment and just look up and giggle. Or at least wonder why a big-nosed bird with a pair of tights on her head is pointing at hand-drawn slides from a pizza-box podium.

I was banned from Twitter for well over five years and returning to it, I see nothing has changed. The same people are looking for tweets and likes, there is a similar roll call of rage and outrage. Perhaps the only subtle shift is the speed at which people are prepared to abandon one outrage and move on to the next. One second they really cared about Ukraine; now all they care about is Palestine. There is no consistency or authenticity in any of it, nothing for anything to anchor itself to. Everyone is tossed around like an unmoored ship on an angry sea.

I post stuff out there without really asking anything of anyone except, sometimes, to consider what they hold to be true, or to laugh at me, or to show support for people I see are being f*cked over by the media or the government or both.

I am particularly keen to try and keep women feeling good about themselves. Not about stupid stuff like hair, make-up or wrinkles, but about what's on the inside, about how tough and bloody brilliant women are at coping with all the stuff they cope with on a daily basis.

Despite this, there is a handful of people who still turn up on my feed purely to be angry or cross, or a combination of the two. My sense is that they arrive angry and cross with the express purpose of being angry and cross at me no matter what comes out of my mouth.

Here's a good example.

I post my blast from the past video of Chris Whitty, encouraging anyone who watches it to cheer up: 'Just for the lols. Have a good weekend, people. Hang in there.'

And among the usual onslaught of kindness from lovely people laughing along, there is this:

@CBibby96: Stop it. This man has and is working helping people in the NHS, considering all the operations you have had with their care there really is no need to mock.

Oh my days. Who called the fun police? There are always these morally superior people who feel the need to rail against fun and point out to me what a mean-arsed, ungrateful twat I am.

And of course, this person has a point. My brain surgery on the NHS saved my life. The NHS has relocated my dislocated arms more than 42 times. It has also rebuilt my daughter's hip and fixed my other daughter's broken leg.

But my gratitude to the genius surgeons and staff that made all this happen (now expressed in the way of charitable donations), and my support of people with epilepsy – these things can be true AT THE SAME TIME as my absolute lack of faith in the man I'm taking the p*ss out of.

We are all capable of holding more than one thought at the same time. Or believing more than one thing at the same time.

I could not have a more profound appreciation for what the team at the Hospital for Neurology did for me. They not only saved my life but gave me a life I could live.

But as for the institution of the NHS, and all the political, financial and lobbying groups and big Pharma and middle management on £250K a year... They all need sweeping out with a big broom.

My reply to Mr @CBibby96? Respectfully, would you mind just fucking off?

The other classic is: 'I don't always agree with you, but you are so right about this.'

Of course, I am always grateful to people who take the time to engage with whatever I am banging on about and it's great that we have found something we agree on.

What's odd is saying 'but you are so right about this'. It implies that when I have a different opinion to their own, I am wrong.

If I am wrong, the individual presumably believes their own opinion is right; and when we agree, we are both right.

I know I have said this plenty of times in the past, but just for old time's sake: we don't have to agree, and when it comes to opinions neither you nor I are the arbiter of what is right and what is wrong.

And all of that is very much okay.

14 September

I am on the road with a suitcase and nowhere to leave it when I need a wee. In these situations you have to make friends fast – and be able to suss out the trustworthiness of strangers pretty quickly, too.

I can say, hand on heart, I wouldn't really give a rat's ass if some random that I have arbitrarily appointed keeper-of-my-stuff decided to walk off with my suitcase. Right this minute I cannot think of a single thing in my luggage I would miss that much or that wouldn't be replaceable. Perhaps my yellow dress, given to me by a fancy friend and well beyond my budget.

But otherwise, good luck to you. A lot of that stuff needs a good wash so you are a braver man than I.

However, if they legged it with my backpack of power, I would officially be in the temporary shit. Passport, money, comms, glasses, MacBook (with the script for my new book) – all gone.

You'd think this would be a good argument for keeping the backpack of power with me, but I don't think you can really ask someone to watch your stuff and then take the important items with you. Feels sort of insulting – like, I trust you with my dirty laundry, but not my valuables.

This seems like the opposite way a hard-nosed woman of the road would operate, and clearly I am not advocating trust in Mexico City, cheap bars, dodgy hotels or other arse-end places where your two most likely outcomes are getting stabbed or raped (or both).

Either way, the man I just made guardian of my bags got chatting. He wanted to know what I was doing here in Miami and what I thought of America. I told him, as I always tell anyone who asks, that America always was and remains the greatest country on the face of the earth. And that Americans are different from all others because they have freedom hardwired into the soul.

He seemed surprised, then kind of pleased with the idea. 'Either freedom or fuck you...' he laughed.

And it is precisely that. Americans are born with this sense that they can. American kids are taught: 'I can, I am, I will,' and they believe it. I think this is all thanks to the Founding Fathers and the Constitution, the single greatest document ever produced. And thanks to generations that have kept alive the principles it enshrines. It also has a great deal to do with the Second Amendment and the Right to Bear arms.

But 'fuck you' is a great way of putting it.

We got to talking about why I was in the States, with me gently trying to explain I was here in support of the January 6 boys who have been given life sentences for the crime of entering the Capitol Building on January 6, 2021 during a massive Trump rally in DC. Many of us involved on that day firmly believe the 'insurgency' into the Capitol building was co-ordinated by those determined to bring Trump down.

The American gentleman didn't know the expression

J6'ers. Or what January 6 was. Or why anyone would be doing anything to do with people who were put in prison for being inside (known as storming) the Capitol Building on that day.

And I was struck by how much we assume things in life. We assume other people know what we know. I often assume people will care about what I care about and I am certain the things I care about should matter to ordinary Americans.

But the hard truth is that they do not.

Outside of my circle of people on the road in the USA, the things that matter so much to me do not matter to a great many people. Many don't have any opinion about the things I feel most strongly about – indeed, some believe the opposite.

'But if you break into a government building you are bound to get punished,' he said, quite rationally.

He is not wrong. Just as I am not right. And just sitting in a bar talking to a stranger kind enough to watch my stuff and share a few laughs with me proves that point with the kind of sharpness that stings like a slap across the face.

It is so important to spend time among those who are the opposite of all that you are, or, at least, who come at life from a completely different perspective.

I am grateful to him for the reminder.

20 September

Ah, the autumn vaccination programme.

It's quite beyond the ability of any rational human

to explain why people who have had 15 boosters, caught COVID three times (they know this because they are still testing every day in the hope of a positive result) and live fairly mundane lives with low-to-zero risk of infection, are so excited that the Autumn Booster Campaign has been announced by the government.

You could feel it coming. Not only because of the brand-new vaccination centres springing up over the summer with zero demand and yet on seemingly endless budgets. But because of the tangible frisson of excitement among the booster mafia about getting yet another opportunity to go through the performance of getting a jab.

Just such a vaccination centre was erected on land adjacent to our favourite farm shop and butcher, which caused much tutting and huffing by my good self. How dare they impose such a monstrosity, and the idiots therein, on a place I very much liked!

I have a sneaky suspicion the savvy landowners who are making a terrific success out of this farm shop, animal enclosure, butcher and bakery enterprise, worked out the many benefits of the arrangement. Local government agencies pay well to put up a building on their land; they bring fibre broadband to the site; and they unlock any awkward future planning applications. Good on the landowners for using the idiots to their advantage! It's a pity it's the taxpayer footing the bill, but all the same.

Lovely Mark and I have stood and watched the morons turning up for their boosters with their bits of paperwork and time allocations. It is cultish, just like a weird church where the lead male bangs all the women and kids, or a Nigerian pastor gets everyone to starve themselves to death in the name of salvation.

Only people with an incredibly warped sense of the world and fear of leaving it can belong in this place. And yet here they all are, in their droves.

I am relieved to see that most are old and partly crippled. Not because it gives me any sense of pleasure to watch old and partly crippled people struggle out of their cars and cross a dirt car park to get more muck put into their arms. But because the young are not here, which reassures me that:

a   they have better things to do with their time, and

b   they aren't buying into this crap any more.

I make a quiet pledge to continue to rip the arse out of these idiotic centres to do my bit for humanity, and return the very next day to film what I think is a HILARIOUS skit at the sign offering Drive-Through Vaccinations.

I stick a 'Would you like fries with that?' poster to the sign, and have a good giggle pretending to be outraged that some little maggot has vandalised the sign and is mocking sensible people getting their booooostaaaa as if they are at a drive-through McDonald's.

When I post it, lots of those commenting think it's a sign from three or four years ago: 'I remember those awful places...' They are unable to believe this was filmed just yesterday and this crap is still going on.

It's a deeply dark thing to know that we lost so many

people to COVID. Not just the ones who were killed off by whatever CHYNA released onto humanity; not just the ones that never made it through lockdowns or who just managed to make it to the other side but will never trust people again – but also those people lost to the cult of COVID in such a way that they cannot leave its injectable embrace because were they to step away from it, step out from its spell, they might see it was all a lie fabricated to deliver profit and (I would argue) weaker hearts, and that is too big a thought for most of these cultists to take on.

25 September

Just when you wonder if people could get any more stupid, some silly twat comes along and chops down one of the loveliest trees: the landmark tree at Sycamore Gap, beside Hadrian's Wall in Northumberland.

It was marked up with paint to highlight where to cut, then apparently cut down in the middle of the night.

The people who know things at the Northumberland National Park Authority believe the tree was 'deliberately felled' in an act of vandalism.

I would just love to get my hands on the 16-year-old kid and his mate who did it. Or at least, got arrested after the event and are likely to have done it.

Because, genuinely, I would like to know why. I mean, of all the things you could do!

Part of me can't help but think they were put up to it by someone with a grudge – some old duffer who was refused planning permission for his house or refused permission to take down some trees in his garden, so as an act of revenge thought he would take down the most photographed tree in the country.

If there were fancy houses nearby, I would say that one of the posh pricks had paid their kids to do it, to improve their view or their sunlight. This often happens in Cornwall when cockwombles with holiday homes want to improve their view; before you know it some ancient oak has suddenly got 'sick' and has to be felled. Or is killed off by a thousand cuts to its trunk and roots.

But at Hadrian's Wall there are no houses nearby.

It is possible that someone with a severe mental illness has a grudge against Robin Hood and, given this is known as Robin Hood's tree, decided to hack it down. This theory is a bit more tenuous, but still.

There are so many odd things about it.

The tree is up a chuffing great hill in the middle of a field, so you would have to haul your chainsaw up there sweating like a fat bloke in Panama. And I don't know if you have ever held a chainsaw and placed it to the trunk of a tree, but it is terrifying. If you don't know what you're doing, and even if you do, it's a blatantly mad act.

The tree is big. You are little. And your head is pretty squishy.

It takes skill and practice and time. And makes a lot of noise.

What the hell? You would only do it if you were really motivated to do it and had true purpose and something to gain, which is why I am not buying the story that it was a

16-year-old kid committing a merry act of vandalism just for kicks.

I believe it was a planned and financed event (of rage, malice or revenge) and someone pretty powerful somewhere knows why.

As it turns out, the gaze of suspicion has fallen on a 69-year-old from the area who has just been evicted from his farm following a long-running dispute with the landowners. He was questioned by police and forced to defend his reputation over the weekend after speculation on social media.

Walter Renwick has told the media he was not the one who cut the tree down.

Walter Renwick is a professional lumberjack.

Mostly I am a bit sad for humans that do this kind of stuff. With all we've got going on in the world, the madness we are surrounded by and ugly things everywhere (see Bradford for details), we need to hold on to the nice stuff, like the jolly tree stretching up to the sky.

In a more comedic aside, a plucky 27-year-old from Newcastle decided that rather than just mourn the historic tree and the gap where it used to be, he would plant a sycamore sapling in its place, just metres away from the stump.

Kieran Chapman, who is from Westerhope in Newcastle, said he had got the tree from a garden centre and taken it to the site to 'try and restore people's faith in humanity'.

It was a sweet gesture and perfectly well intended but

the National Trust was having none of it.

A National Trust spokesperson said: 'We understand the strength of feeling following the events at Sycamore Gap this week – and are grateful for the many offers of support and good wishes we've received from near and far. It's important for everyone to remember that the site is a scheduled ancient monument and a globally important archaeological setting, with UNESCO world heritage designation, and that altering or adding to it can damage the archaeology, and is unlawful without prior consent from government.'

The National Trust dug up Kieran Chapman's young sycamore.

Blah blah blah, boring boring boring, rules, red tape, bureaucracy, bollocks. Nothing crushes humanity more than people who come along and dig up saplings in defence of an area where a bloody great tree used to be, in order to 'preserve the ancient monument'.

I applaud that young chap for his initiative. I urge the National Trust to stop being such pompous arses. And I hope the miserable git who felled the giant sycamore suffers some ignoble end, at a time he least expects it.

29 September

Knowing when to keep my mouth shut has clearly always been an issue for me, as both my father and mother have been at great pains to point out over the last few decades. Memorable examples would be getting deported from Australia for refusing to keep my mouth shut in my quarantine prison and speaking out against the tyranny of the government.

Last night a chatty man at a bar launched into his proud history as a Polish man, avowing that despite actually being a Canadian, his true love is Poland and its political party, the Law and Order Party.

Courtesy of my life on the road among those who are fighting the good fight, I happen to know one of the main figures of that party pretty well. I suggested the Canadian do a little video telling him how marvellous he is. Sometimes my commitment to the cause extends to massaging the egos of those who enjoy that sort of thing.

As I was listening to the Canadian babble on in Polish to make this video, I became slightly obsessed by the way he enunciated his words. Pretty soon Dr Hopkins here (self-promoted) decided the man was deaf, and that he had worked out a way to compensate for his deafness by mimicking how those able to hear, speak.

Having made my diagnosis, I began to speak more clearly and move my lips more obviously to make his job of lip-reading easier – to be a good egg. Sometimes my belief in my uncanny ability to understand and help people extends well beyond my reach.

Emboldened by my extraordinary powers (and perhaps my third Merlot), I asked him if he minded me asking him a personal question. He said no, somewhat too keenly, so I asked, 'Are you deaf?'

And I learned a few things pretty fast. As young people might say, fuck about and find out.

I found out he was not deaf.

I found out young, relatively attractive men do not like to be asked if they are deaf.

And I found out that once asked, a question cannot be unasked, and no amount of honest explanation will assist you in restoring your former image as quite a nice old bird with a good sense of humour.

I will write this here, as I did not have the opportunity to make things right in person (the man with excellent hearing left the bar). I apologise unreservedly for the offence I clearly caused. I should not have assumed you were deaf. I should not have asked if you were deaf. And in future I will assume all men at bars who speak a bit oddly nevertheless have perfect hearing, unless they tell me otherwise.

Christ alive, it's tough being me.

30 September

As I speak, a man next to me in the airport is forcing enough Burger King to feed half of Africa into his face with such speed that he is half gagging, half choking his way through his meal. He may as well just empty that brown bag into a trough and plant his full face into it for all the noise he is making.

I am trying to channel the best version of myself so I imagine he has been very busy, is very tired on the road, and perhaps just worked a night shift.

But my best self is strongly overridden by a much less polite version of me that just wants to tell him to f*ck off and sit somewhere else. There must be about 80% of the seats in this terminal sitting empty and yet Ape Man has chosen to occupy the seat beside mine to jam his face full of burger and fries, licking and slapping away at his greasy fingers like this place isn't one giant bowl of piss and syphilis.

'Just fuck off, and once you are there keep going,' nearly comes out of my mouth, but I settle for turning my back to avoid bringing up my coffee and to signal to him that he is an animal and I am outraged.

I have this relentless, daily optimism about humanity, because it helps me stay sane and doing what I do. But it is moments like this that make me question my beliefs. Many of our species are in fact filthy bastards and I am not certain I would be able to raise a tear if this particular man's plane failed to reach its final destination.

A good friend of mine who used to be very involved with weapons says that some people just aren't worth the oxygen.

He's not wrong.

OCTOBER

2 October

A woman was arrested and charged for masturbating on a public beach.

According to the witness she laid out her towel, got a 'lewd' sex toy from her bag and proceeded to use it on herself, moaning and groaning as she did so.

The witness also took a video of the woman and gave it to the police, who quickly located said woman at a nearby restaurant and arrested her.

When the police asked to search her bag, she admitted to using a vibrator to relax because she was 'stressed', saying that it only took her 20 seconds to orgasm. The woman was then handcuffed and escorted from the beach.

Footage of the encounter has had more than 2.5 million views on social media since it emerged on Friday.

The woman was charged with indecent exposure and disorderly conduct.

Police said the woman, Ms Revels-Glick, apologised while being booked for indecent exposure and disorderly conduct, telling officers she didn't think anyone had seen her.

She was released shortly after her arrest on subpoena, the police report stated.

According to Atlanta-based attorneys Conaway and Strickler, Revels-Glick could face a 12-month jail sentence for 20 seconds of self-gratification. It remains unclear whether she appeared before the courts. 'The state of Georgia aggressively prosecutes people charged with indecent exposure', the attorneys' website reads.

You know what I love about this chick?

For starters, she looks terrific in a one-piece swimsuit, and how many other young women are out there on beaches rocking a lovely one-piece? Everywhere you look there are mountains of flesh strangulated by cheap-ass bikinis, thongs cutting in like a cheese wire on brie.

Second up, her immediate response to the officers detaining her was to re-enact what she was doing and offer up the explanation that she was 'stressed out'. Top bird. What else are you going to do on a family Thanksgiving vacation on the beach when you are feeling a bit uptight? Obviously you're going to whip out your vibrator and wang one off into the breeze to help you be a nicer person for your relatives.

I just love the idea that after a family bust-up it is perfectly sensible to go off and have a how's-your-father until you feel more calm. However, I would add a general advisory to all of us, that if you encounter the police or are questioned by them or detained, you should not begin a full re-enactment of what you think they want to know. Do nothing, say nothing, and act like you have no clue what they are talking about.

My final point about this lovely lady trying to meet her needs, albeit in public, is to repeat that the clip of her being detained has been viewed over 2.5 million times as at the time of writing. Her strongest defence is that an entire country the size of Ireland wants to watch her getting down and dirty on a beach.

To charge someone with indecency or a public order offence when so many of the public are clearly desperate to watch her in action seems like a misallocation of public resources at best, at worst a complete invasion of her life.

And if by some minor miracle you are the officer who put handcuffs on this fine woman in order to parade her from the beach in front of the gawping mouth-breathers with nothing better to do, as if she were some violent hoodlum who might threaten your safety, and you are reading this book – I would like to say that you disgust me far, far more than anything that wonderful woman may or may not have been doing with her own body.

Imagine cuffing a lady just for grinding one out on the shoreline. What were you scared of? Did you think she was going to reach down into her labia without warning and start banging another one out even as you tried to arrest her? Take it from this old hag, that's not how women work. One and done is how most of us function. And if you can achieve that in 20 seconds, it shows just how much you have got your sh*t together in life. Multitasking is not something women take lightly.

If, on the other hand, Ms Revels-Glick is reading this (excellent name, by the way), I say hold your head up high, girl! You look excellent in swimwear (which is more than most can say), you understand your needs and how to fulfil them in 20 seconds (which is a skill in itself), and millions of people want to watch you at it.

You cannot be shamed unless you decide to be. Own it. Be it. And go make all the cash you can out of this moment in the sunshine.

Lots of people are just jealous of you, and most of them don't know where their bits are and certainly have not used them in too long – which is why they are taking videos of you on a beach, the sad little perverts.

Shoulders back, tits up and you do you, girlie.

15 October

I've been thinking a lot about Ms Revels-Glick the last few days. Not in a sexual way (I have yet to get into my lesbian years but they can be only mere moments away), but because her story is a hideously perfect example of how shame works.

Shame is in fact a masterful deception and misunderstood by almost everyone.

Shame isn't a spontaneous feeling. It is cast on to someone, like a net. When a gaggle of ignorant men gathers to throw rocks at a woman, what they are doing is throwing shame at her and, in the process, elevating themselves.

As they throw the shame they feel lighter and better about themselves because they are offloading their own guilts onto the woman.

As they throw the shame they feel more secure because, look at all these other grim-looking men who have gathered to throw shame as well! Each man there would far rather fit in with his fellow miserable cretins than be the lonely woman having rocks thrown at her head. Who would want to be her? Even if you know she is probably quite a nice lady, you aren't going anywhere near her now – or ever, for that matter. Best leave well alone.

And then crowds gather, at first to watch the men throwing rocks and launching shame, and then to join in.

Which is exactly what happened in our fabulous age of social media when one cretin filmed a woman pleasuring herself on a beach, and millions and millions of others dived in to have their say.

They said: 'Imagine doing that in public!' and 'She should be ashamed of herself!' just to elevate themselves, to prove they would never do such a thing, to signal to the clique they want to be accepted by that they are nothing like that terrible woman on the beach.

When it comes to shaming there is so very little difference between maniacal Arabs hurling rocks at a woman's head, and the women with their manicures and pedicures doing the same on Instagram or wherever.

All of them are actually involved in the same thing – casting shame onto another in order to make themselves feel more 'pure', to elevate themselves and, critically, to be accepted by the mob in order that the spotlight NEVER falls on them.

Because here's the thing.

Every single one of those beach-goers who sat, mouth agog, as Christina Revels-Glick was handcuffed and marched from the beach in her swimmers, has pleasured themselves at some point, on their own, in their bedroom or perhaps somewhere altogether more exciting like on a plane.

Every single person enjoying the shame of Christina has done exactly as she has done (just not necessarily on a public beach) and every single one of the shamers publicly acts as if they would never do such a thing.

Self-pleasuring is the weirdest secret ever. As is sex generally in America. You try even mentioning the subject as part of a funny routine and many will wipe the laughter off their face because they can't be seen to acknowledge that sex is a thing, even as they are surrounded by ten of their own bloody children.

I'd argue a great many of these mouth-breathing Shakers could do with wanking themselves silly for a good six months just to lighten the hell up and realise that pleasure is not a sin and that we all need it.

And while the mob salivates over the enjoyable act of casting shame on others and hiding their own failings (or the fact they spanked one out this very morning before breakfast), all they are really doing is blending in with the serpent, becoming part of it, a single, oily scale on the back of something incredibly hard to control or placate. Menacing, lurking, the snake can strike anyone at any time – so much safer to cling to the back of this poisonous, slithering thing than be out there alone trying to face it down.

Addition to October, written in December 2023

It's strange how one woman's story stays with you.

Think of all the noise you are surrounded by, in your own home, from the worldly things you are a part of, from the frenzy of social media and the news and all the rest of it. There is a cacophony of noise raging around your ears at all times.

And yet, Christina's story stayed with me, fine and clear like a little piccolo shrilling out above a mighty orchestra.

Now I know why. Christina didn't make it. This is an excerpt from the story that followed:

Liberty County Coroner confirmed Revels-Glick had been dead for approximately 30 days before her body was found in a rented apartment in Hinesville, Georgia, in which she had been living.

They said, 'It took a while to figure out who she was, but they managed to work it out because she had bought her son a motorbike and she'd filled out the registration paperwork, so they had that.'

They added, 'When they told us, we thought, "Well at least we know where she's at now."'

The death certificate and police incident report appear to shed light on a sad story: Revels-Glick shot herself in the head and died of a wound that appears not to have been immediately fatal.

Instead, her landlady found her decomposing remains in the middle of a horrific scene of blood splatters and trails after entering the apartment because Revels-Glick had failed to pay rent.

The Hinesville Police Department report states that a pistol was found lying on the master bedroom bed. It notes, 'A hole was also observed in the roof directly above the bed. On the opposite side of the hallway a decomposing female body (later identified as Ms Christina Revels-Glick) was observed laying on the ground.'

Officer Timothy Conley wrote that there was 'a large amount of blood' on the living room floor, 'two separate blood trails leading in both directions in the hallway,' and 'blood [was] observed in the guest bedroom on a chair, desk and computer'.

The report notes that Revels-Glick had 'an exit wound from a bullet on her forehead'.

There is a much darker side to this story than even this.

In the weeks that followed, troubled neighbours came forward wanting the real truth to be heard. They are certain Christina didn't kill herself. They are sure from the noises they heard from the apartment the night before it all went quiet for the last time, that a menacing boyfriend had killed Christina. His car was there on the night of the fight; they heard strange noises coming from the apartment when he was there. And then he was never seen again.

None of us is in a position to play roving investigator, and I am sure none of us want to. But even the most cursory glance at the paperwork and pictures from the apartment show that nothing adds up: the bloody handprints on the walls and desperate trails of blood in two directions in the hallway speak of someone trying to save themselves after being shot. The exit wound in the forehead but the bullet mark in the ceiling above the bed; the boyfriend never found or questioned…

Yet no one even dusted the gun found on the bed for prints. The officer filing his findings even got the year wrong on his report.

Christina's last moments were ones of absolute trauma and speak of a woman trying to save herself, clawing for help with bloodied hands, regardless of who fired that weapon.

And more sad even than a woman who couldn't reach help when she was fatally wounded, and whose body gave up on her before her big old heart ever did, is the apparent fact that others had given up on her long before.

She lay there in a pool of her own blood for more than thirty days and the reason she was found was not because she was loved, but because her rent was due. Even in death someone still wanted something from her.

You know, it's easy to romanticise these moments. It's easy for me to paint a picture entirely from Christina's side because her story always called to my heart and I am a willing champion for those who are kicked into the gutter; I have lain there alongside them.

If you like a life of drink or drugs or wild decisions, I am sure there comes a point at which your family washes its hands of you. There is no blame to be thrown around here; none of us gets to be an angel just because we are dead.

But I am sad that she is gone. And nothing in that apartment says she killed herself even though it's easier for the police to just file it away as a suicide. Much neater and cleaner, and far less resource-intensive. After all, if her own family didn't care that she was dead for a month, why should the police? Why bother dusting the gun for prints and finding an inconvenient set that shouldn't have been there? Why check the date when you are just dotting the i's and crossing the t's on a report for a woman no one cared about – especially one caught winking on a beach a few months earlier.

And that's the bit that really gets me: how women, especially women, are so disposable. And that their lives can be so reduced by shame, by others casting aspersions, that their death ceases to matter.

Sometimes I just want to hit rewind on life, like you used to be able to do with those clunky old VHS tape players. You held your finger on the rewind button and watched the stuff you'd just seen fly backwards past your face in super-speedy time, undoing everything you had just viewed, undoing unkindness.

I'd love to be on that beach with the weirdo watching Christina pleasuring herself, reaching for his phone to film her. And I would love to break his hands.

'Don't you even think about it!' I'd hiss in his ear, and advise him to walk away quietly before I did something worse to his tiny, stiff excuse for a penis.

Who knows if it would have saved her?

No one can say if Christina's global shaming was the trigger that led to her death, driving her to kill herself or become so vulnerable she was able to be killed.

But I can say for certain that when you are in the eye of the storm, ending your life seems like a very rational way to make the noise go away.

I never knew Christina but somehow she stays with me still. If I could perform one final act for her, I'd show the world a video of every one of those women in the fancy restaurant who gawped like guppies as Christina was shackled from the beach, and every voyeur who clicked on the link of the video of Christina masturbating. I'd show a video of them dry-humping their own pillow, or getting off on some rubbery pink thing they 'got given by a friend'.

Even the momentary threat of it would be enough for a hot, dry sweat to creep onto their collar and a prickling bead of it to slide quietly from under their perfect boobs.

I'd like them to feel that fear.

Because, of course, throwing shame is an action without consequence. No woman in a sandy hole ever throws the rock back at the men intent on her death. No Christina ever gets to insult those who so insulted her.

There is just me, or us. Calling it out – quietly and repeatedly – until someone hears.

The hashtag #BeKind often trends when someone is being publicly shamed, particularly when it's another powerful male paedophile. But this too is part of an elaborate illusion. What better way to try and fit in with the cretins than to self-elevate with a hashtag that says you are one of the 'kind people' who would never shame a single soul?

We are all Christina. All it takes is one decision or unfortunate moment to set us on a path from which we are never coming back.

The best we can promise is to never join in the shaming of another, whether by throwing stones or by using a frigging hashtag that lies about #BeingKind.

Much has changed in this one chapter of my life since I first wrote it, and yet my view on the world remains constant. And I say to you, Christina, now freed from this place that was never enough to contain you, exactly what I said when I first heard your name:

If you are reading this, Ms Revels-Glick (excellent last name, by the way), I say hold your head up high, girl. You look excellent in swimwear (which is more than most can say), you understand your needs and how to fulfil them in 20 seconds (which is a skill in itself), and millions of people want to watch you at it.

You cannot be shamed unless you decide to be. Own it. Be it. And go make all the cash you can out of this moment in the sunshine.

Lots of people are just jealous of you, and most of them don't know where their bits are and certainly have not used them in too long – which is why they are taking videos of you on a beach, the sad little perverts.

Shoulders back, tits up and you do you, girlie.

NOVEMBER

2 November

Given I am a little bit known and have a distinctly more recognisable face than ever thanks to the youngsters on TikTok and the fact that everyone else who is a bit known has chosen their noses out of a catalogue – given these things, some might imagine my life to be an endless parade of well-organised, well-maintained efficiency involving staff, security and an army of engaged and industrious cleaners.

Quite the opposite is true, of course.

When I rock up to do a speech at say, the Oxford Union, they typically ask how many of my team are coming along, or how many of my security team will be in attendance.

And the answer is, they don't exist.

The team that I am thrilled to be surrounded by is a much more haphazard affair involving one man and a cluster of excellent human beings who have fallen into my path.

I am a bit like one of those Venus Fly Traps; if you

trip anywhere near me you might find yourself stuck there forever with me slowly feeding off you until you pass out or give up on life altogether.

The main anchor of this non-existent team is Lovely Mark, now somewhat legendary on the road, often referred to and loved without hesitation by everyone that meets him.

Lovely Mark, as you well know but I like to labour the point, is my husband. He is also the bloke I was caught having sex with in a field, back in the days when I was young, carefree and way more equipped to deal with gravity than I am now. When I am being criticised by the mediocre with limited research skills about being a harlot for shagging a married man in a field, I silence them by reminding them, as I do, that he is my husband. It blows their tiny brains that someone might actually want to do that kind of thing with their own husband. Such is their limited universe.

In truth, of course, he was someone else's husband at the time, and that kind of behaviour was frowned upon by the wife in question, for good reason. I have to say that when the same thing happened to me with my first husband, I kind of frowned upon it too.

Americans have this great concept of passing kindness along, of 'paying it forward'. For example, in a queue (or line) you would pay for coffee for someone behind you in the line, or leave money at a cash desk to pay for someone else's shopping.

I am not certain that my first husband having multiple

sexual affairs and then me going on to do the same to some poor other woman is exactly the kind of 'paying it forward' Conservative Americans would approve of. But in a malevolent kind of way I see there are parallels, even if they are uncomfortable ones.

Lovely Mark is 'the man who can' for my stand-up / comedy career-that-I-never-saw-coming-but-which-was-perhaps-always-in-my-bones-somewhere. He is the one who built the website and learned how to sell tickets online. He is the one who can engage with theatre managers and has the tenacity to secure bookings and sign contracts.

And he is the one who has quietly built up relationships over long periods such that we have become trusted and everyone works together in the truest sense. Without him there is no me, and I say that without humour or hesitation.

He is not perfect. Sometimes I want to stab him repeatedly with a blunt butter knife for being so bloody OCD. Like when he goes into the dustbin to retrieve a recyclable item I have thrown away and takes it back to the sink, like a father making a child go back and pick up their litter. I threw away the shitty plastic tub covered in creamy crap FOR A REASON.

And that reason was that I could not in any way be arsed to clean the bastard thing and therefore took the adult decision to send it to landfill. And I am perfectly fine with that.

I mean, I am nearly 50, for fuck's sake! I may make it to 55, I may not, and honestly (without self-pity), I am not planning for it. So if I can save myself five minutes in exchange for one shitty bit of plastic sitting in landfill for a few decades, I am A-okay with that.

But Lovely Mark is not. And he will fish it out and rinse it out and make a great deal of noise about it and sigh heavily to indicate that he is literally living with a monster and I should be ashamed of myself. I am not. I am only ashamed that I am married to the kind of man that checks what I put in the bin. Stalky perv bin-rumbler.

It is also bloody annoying that he is called Lovely Mark, even though I gave him that name, because it is now how a legion of ladies also refer to him on the road. 'Ah, he's so lovely!' they tell me, oblivious to his bin rummaging or propensity to leave his socks on the floor next to the bed in case he fancies wearing them again tomorrow.

'You are so lucky to have him,' they say. And I grimace and nod and agree. Because what choice do I have?

Lucky, lucky?! You call it lucky to be married to a man who in times of deep personal crisis (me in tears about something trivial) will first stop to tidy the cutlery drawer before offering me any attention or sympathy whatsoever? You think it's lucky to be married to a dude who is obsessed with milk being in the fridge at all times and who measures out his yoghurt and adds frozen raspberries to it the night before in preparation for his meagre breakfast the next day AND thinks cleaning a toilet involves swishing bleach around the inside rim a couple of times? You call that lucky, you daft moos?

He's even starting to use his fame, would you believe it? Lovely Mark is literally coasting on my coat tail and celebrity status for his personal benefit and I am still the one supposed to be grateful and praising the Lord for having bestowed on me such a blessing? (NB: For my American readers, this is sarcasm. I do not mean this literally. It is important to me that you understand dry wit.)

He went to a regional airport recently and tried to check in his bag with a budget airline.

I don't know if you have ever endured flying a budget airline from a regional airport, but there are two important things to know. First, you will be penalised for daring to try and fly anywhere from a regional airport, and secondly you will be raped for your cash at every turn by the budget airline, whether it's for seating, luggage, food, basic sanitation or the avoidance of indignity. Whatever happens, you will pay and you will spunk your cash like a black rapper making a music video.

But not Lovely Mark, oh no.

He rocks up at the EasyJet check-in without having printed his own boarding pass and without having given them three years' notice that he intended to bring one small check-in bag – two cardinal sins with a budget airline, both requiring that you remortgage your house to atone for.

But Lovely Mark just looks at the guy and says, 'I wonder if you can help me.'

The guy sees he is called Mark, recognises his face (no one has ever seen Lovely Mark and he never shows his face, ever) and says, 'Wait a minute, you're Lovely Mark, aren't you?'

And checks-in him and his bag for free.

For free! Can you even imagine? If that had been me, I would have been left sobbing at the check-in desk, desperately trying to destroy my own luggage and insert the most embarrassing bits of grey underwear into my pockets or shove a whole shampoo up my vag. But not lovely Mark. For he must be wafted on board by ostrich feathers because he has to tolerate that old cow, Katie Hopkins.

It seriously takes the piss.

However. Regardless of the humiliations I am forced to endure because of being in the presence of Lovely Mark, the benefits of him being around are many and it is true that he is the most important part of the team and actually way more important to the tour than me.

I may be the monkey but it's his circus and he is the circus master.

Having said all that, it's this little monkey that has to write an entire show, tell people she is funny (while not really being certain whether others actually find this to be true), sweat her little monkey nuts off on stage trying to remember what she wanted to say, and not piss herself or make a complete dick of herself to the point that people walk out.

This little monkey sometimes wonders about her life choices, let me tell you.

Lovely Mark is the team. And he is tremendous. Even when I want to spatula him to death for bring an anal freak (not literally – although there have been moments...), I always know and trust that he has complete faith in what I am trying to do. And because of that faith everything will be okay. And that's quite a remarkable thing.

The rest of the team is a motley crew of the self-employed, never officially employed, or angel volunteers who see something that needs doing and decide the way they join in this revolution we are building towards is to lend their talents and their time.

The tech boys that we tour with are two of my favourite people on the planet and give Lovely Mark a run for his money. As with all the best things in life, I met them quite by chance and we struck up a bond over my deep admiration for what they had just achieved, their attitude and their willingness to go buy me a beer.

It was 2018, and Fiona and the gang had organised a remarkable Freedom Rally in Trafalgar Square. There was proper staging, a terrific tech screen, and sound – three things most protests fail at spectacularly.

I'm not sure where the funding for all of this came from, and truly that's a question best left unasked. But the cost of that event was massive.

I hadn't been asked to speak (I will explain why in mere moments) but that's not why I attend such things anyway. It's odd to me how many of the 'faces' of a movement only attend if they are speaking; unless they have the attention and the stage they seem to feel there is no point in them being there.

I think the opposite. If decent, ordinary people can find the time and money to get together with others to feel better together, then it is surely the job and the privilege of those who are a little bit known to be among the family cheering them on.

I typically walk the very outer edge of these events, feeling the feel of being part of this glorious crowd and giving out the odd cuddle or sneaky pic if anyone spots my nose under my hat and recognises me.

Word spread pretty fast that I was there and the amazing crowd somehow had me thrust up on stage and speaking without me having much say in the matter. I scrambled with the amazing tech boys to sort some music, I got a brief grip of what I was trying to do, and I jumped out on stage. Short shorts, scrappy shirt, boots and a whole lot of love for these amazing people.

When I came off stage and thanked the boys that had made the sound work at this scale, they offered to buy me a beer and sent one of their team to go find one. And that was that. I found my tech team on the day I turned up at a Freedom Rally and ended up on stage, and we've been working together ever since.

I truly believe it is the people who attend, the people who organise and the people who invest their energy in bringing the crowd together who really matter. The person in the spotlight so rarely does. It's a real joy to share that same feeling with the team that now helps me on the road across the UK.

I don't think of my gig as 'selling tickets'. It feels more like sending out invitations to be part of a brilliant gathering of friends, and we work together to cover the cost of making that happen.

I am rarely inclined to discuss those who are not 'on team', firstly because we should never shoot inside the tent. Any time we are criticising our own we are facing the wrong direction. There are always bigger and more deserving enemies out there on the 'left' and among the 'globalists' than there are on our side.

But there are those inside our tent whose only reason for being there is themselves. And they bother me. Self-preservation is their everything – and self-preservation is what leads to the loss of entire peoples.

Self-preservation means others on the side of 'freedom' see me as a contaminant'. The fact I have been so universally and extremely cancelled from everything leads them to fear being seen with me. They certainly do not want to share a stage with me. Not out of principle, though they will claim this is the case. Not because of what I say, because most of them will never have actually listened. But purely because if they appear with me, the same cancellation might happen to them.

The logic trail for the left is:
- Katie Hopkins is a racist who has been rightfully cancelled.
- You appeared with her on stage.
- You are a racist who must be cancelled as well.

The logic trail for the self-preservation boys is:
- If I appear with Katie, I will be cancelled.

- I will refuse to appear with her to preserve myself.
- I will say I won't appear with her in order to earn credit at the places I can perform.

It's disturbing and perfectly true and applies to most of the boys. Particular offenders worthy of a mention are Andrew Doyle, Alastair Williams, Nigel Farage, Toby Young… The list goes on.

They are Free Speech defenders, as long it is their own speech they are defending. Which, of course, is not how this thing works at all.

What I am certain of is that to be an absolutist like me, and to have been eviscerated and fought my way back with their feet on my head, is a far more powerful thing than still to be tiptoeing about trying to tread the line finely enough that you avoid being removed. They have never once provided any support to me. And I am so grateful that I have never looked to them for it.

It is my audience, ordinary people, who lift me up. And far better that than the slippery boys who wouldn't know a pair of balls if a pair hit them on the chin. Which is how I assume they spend their free time: blowing each other.

10 November

I do wonder about the relationship I have with my dogs.

On no other planet, in no other life and certainly not in this one would I willingly invest so much time, energy, care and attention into another life form, be it a husband, a child or some infatuation. And yet this couple of extraordinarily expensive dogs has not only infiltrated my life and consumed much of it – they get away with the kind of crap no one would ever pull off and survive in any other circumstance.

I actually think dogs may be evil master manipulators, like those men you read about in the Daily Mail that act normal on the outside but fully abuse their wives and control their every move, from how they speak and dress to how they spend their time.

That's the dogs and me. I now have to dress like a tramp in their company for fear of being muddied, molested or secretly chomped full of holes. When I am with them they control where I go because they like to run free anywhere there are rivers or rabbits or preferably both. And I daren't spend too much time talking to anyone or any other dog because Tilda will get her spine up and engage menacing-protector mode.

On a recent walk I took a fall – which is more common than you might think because I don't have total control or ownership over my left leg and foot any more, and they tend to do their own thing when unsupervised.

If you have fallen recently as an adult, you will be aware that it is very different to falling as a child. As an adult there are at least two hours between the moment of the trip and the impact with the ground. In this time you get to think about your life, how much it is going to hurt when you land, and whether you will dislocate something or possibly shatter a whole tooth.

Upon landing, I was working out whether any of said possibilities had occurred, and concerned with how many people had seen my spectacular slump into the mud, when Tilda Dog decided to helpfully run at my prostrated form and engage extreme-shag mode.

Despite the fact I am missing half my skull, which leaves my brain open to the elements save a thin covering of skin and hair, and had just taken a fall and was lying flat in the mud, my dog, who I lavish with affection on a daily basis, decided this was the perfect moment to grab both my ears and start humping my brain like a randy donkey bumming its mate.

a   Tilda is female.

b   I am not big on being humiliated.

c   If the stupid mutt thinks she is my protector, why does she start humping my brain when I am clearly in some physical distress?

And it's this behaviour that has me wondering. All these TikTok and Insta types are full of praise for these creatures, bleating on about how they are man's best friend, the most loyal friend you will ever know. But not once in my adult life has any friend, husband or child immediately starting shagging my ear when I was in trouble.

I am reminded that my little daughter India once asked me, 'What's for tea?' when I took a very nasty fall off my bike and was lying in a tangle of metal and skin in the road. But she is massively autistic so must be forgiven for not knowing it was not the best time to ask.

26 November

My dad was born on 26 November 1946.

That's a pretty weird thing to think about now that we are in 2023. Father always tells everyone he is well past his sell-by date, is very clear that he does not want to be resuscitated, and will not stand for flowers or a fancy coffin at his funeral.

It's funny to think that even in death Father's menace will prevent us from burying him in anything other than a chipboard oblong without a single primrose. The begrudging curmudgeonliness of it all will rather suit him, I suppose.

As for the DNR notice that father says he wants tattooed on his chest, he may not be so lucky. Mother says it is not Dad's choice to make and while he might want to be left to die in peace, she needs him back and will get people to make their best effort to revive him.

Mum has very limited patience for Dad's ageing ways, and when she considers his inevitable demise, she imagines herself into the role of some kind of Florence Nightingale, prepared not only to bring him back to life but presumably to nurse him through his new state of back-from-the-deadness, regardless of any horrors that might entail.

I am making light of all this in the pure nervous certainty that one day, not too far from now, I will lose my parents to the other side, and I have no idea how I will ever cope with that. By making light of it I am kidding myself that perhaps it won't happen. Or that I am distanced enough from it to survive intact.

I will not. It will be terrible.

But for now I still have both of them and Father keeps on getting older and a little less pleasant and more forgetful and controlling of Mother.

I have to hope that the end comes before the brain gives up. I fear the day I get the call to say that he has been found naked in aisle 6 of Lidl armed with a bread knife. (I am not certain which bit of this scenario would be most mortifying.) Perhaps the only happy thing about the elderly when they reach this stage is that they have no idea about it at all.

Right now Father is stoically preparing himself for more difficult times ahead. He has purchased one of those recliner chairs that literally goes flat to the point of becoming a bed, but can also lift you up and out of your chair into the standing position. It is quite remarkable to watch.

My sister hates it. She thinks it is something Dad has no need of yet and it makes her heart sad because it is something she associates with the very end of life.

I think it is terrific and only wish I could speed up the settings so that it ejected my father with the kind of rapidity usually reserved for fighter pilots in faulty planes. We could press the button and eject him out of it at speed if he was refusing to get up or being particularly obtuse that day.

He has had (and, I would argue, is still having) a very good life, and in his quieter moments must be very proud of himself for making it from a tiny council house on the wrong side of the water, shared with two huge brothers, provided for solely by their own work and that of my Granny, to owning his own terrifically modern house and living well past the number of years any other members of his family ever saw.

Theirs was an excellent time to be alive and to live through. And his is a life well lived. Even if he remains ridiculously stubborn in all regards and refuses to have his heating on properly, has to have things done his way, and imagines that leaving his stairs uncarpeted is going to end well.

We tried to have this conversation with the Mothership the other day. I told her that her granddaughter and aspiring nurse says her stairs should be carpeted for safety. Mother went into an enormous sulk and suggested that if we hire a carpetfitter, she will lock the door and refuse to let him in. And then she uttered the immortal Mother line, 'Why can't we just wait until we fall first?'

I am uncertain of the logic behind this, but I suspect from a Methodist point of view it means that if you fall and break something and endure pain and hardship, then you have earned the right to spend some money on yourself to try and make things a bit better.

Old people. What can I tell you? Other than that old people who moan about even older people and how selfish they are never recognise those same traits in themselves.

In truth, I hope I pop off before either of them so I don't have to face any time when they aren't around. I am not sure I am grown up enough to handle any aspect of losing them.

DECEMBER

3 December

In the Family Hopkins preparations are already underway for the Big Day.

Over the years this has come to mean a multitude of things – all exactly the same each year but somehow never called out directly by any gobby member of the family because the whole month is dedicated to two things: keeping the peace and having a good day.

I for one am not at all certain there is any peace to be kept. There are always hostilities shimmering right beneath the surface of any proper family in which the members are completely different one from another but chance has it they share a last name and an unspoken history of what a woke teenager of today might describe as child abuse.

My sister is an aficionado of not committing to anything until around 20 December. For all the years I can remember she 'might be working over Christmas'. Due to the reverence and esteem in which the elders of my clan hold doctors and anyone that moves in their orbit, her excuse is accepted without question as a noble and valiant act of self-giving to the nation's health service.

I could say a few things here but won't in the interests of keeping the peace and not wanting to detract from having a good day.

Then again…

Firstly, my sister is in fact a pharmacist, not an emergency consultant for brain injuries or a surgeon specialising in exploded body organs. The idea that every year since adulthood a pharmacist has been required to be on 10-minute standby at the hospital to hand out the odd paracetamol is clearly ridiculous. As is the yearly miracle when, on the 23rd, it turns out she isn't working over Christmas after all.

This allows her and her offshoots to avoid the preparations, the finding of holiday accommodation or commitment to anything due to the fact that she might have been working. But because she is my sister and in the orbit of the people giving life-saving care to the ungrateful masses, we must all say nothing and not even make a joke about it, ever.

When my sister does rock up, she does incredibly useful things like create cheesecakes and peel 40,000 carrots at 6am and she keeps herself generally busy somewhere tidying something. So I am guessing it is the commitment in advance that she actually hates, because she seems to quite like the whole jamboree itself. Perhaps it is a way of preserving her sanity, and as you will know by now – if you know me at all – I believe preserving one's sanity is everything.

5 December

I woke up this morning with a slight sense of foreboding about Christmas Day which bugged me until I had eaten four crumpets and had a shower to get myself going.

Respecting the December tradition of keeping the peace is always fraught with hazard. We are the Israel / Hamas of the West Country (without the side order of marauding Arabs and suggestions of genocide).

Mother and Father have very particular ideas about how things should be done and, naturally, there is hell to pay for any deviations.

This hell can come in the form of a prolonged period of Mother formally 'not speaking' (usually to me) or a full-on blazing bawl-out between Mother and Father. Either way, there is a current of tension and malevolence that hangs over the month as consideration is given to trying to do things the way that Mother and Father think they should be done.

In more recent years Mum has taken to exclaiming quite at random, 'I sometimes wonder what all the fuss is about! I mean, it's only a day, isn't it? Your father and I would be quite happy on our own. It's just a day like any other.'

Do not be fooled. She is saying this but in no way does she mean this. The idea of them sitting alone on Christmas Day while their selfish offspring do what the

hell they like with their equally selfish grandchildren
– well, that would be an act from which Mum would
never recover. Secretly she looks forward to it all like a
little kid.

Mumsie's way of showing she cares is by feeding. And
that's also part of why Christmas has to happen and must
happen, so she can show she does actually care and be
surrounded by all the good people she cares for. There is
also some oneupmanship in this, which involves sending
pictures to our closest relatives to show how happy and
successful our family is. The fact we are all studiously
dedicated to keeping the peace and having our one good
day is neither here nor there.

The other important part of having a good day is the
hunting down of the perfect pterodactyl to feed us all for
at least eight meals over the period during which peace
must be kept.

Our turkey is no ordinary turkey, oh no. Our turkey
must be foraged in the manner of a wild boar snuffling for
truffles around some damp and fronded forest.

Our turkey must have been fed only on grass or things
turkeys find in the wild, and be still alive on a nice farm
in the arse-end of nowhere mere moments before being
caught and having its neck wrung in a swift and decisive
manner by a farmer with hands the size of dinner plates.

Most importantly, our turkey must have the kind of
body weight formerly only seen on the extremely obese
awaiting gastric-band surgery or those injecting Ozempic
by the litre straight into their eyeballs.

Size is everything. In the days leading up to the good day our mighty fallen bird, now plucked naked on the massive turkey tray, will resemble a small, greying child curled up in the foetal position.

I believe this is the same tray that has been used for sledding in the past, but I may have embellished that for the sake of comedy.

If ever there were some apocalyptic event, I feel pretty certain the Christmas turkey tray would provide decent shelter for the family to get us through the first couple of weeks.

Regardless, the turkey is a beast of beauty and we must all respond with compliments and gasps of wonderment. Much like the birth of baby Jesus, I guess. The avian equivalent of the Nativity scene.

There have been turkey disasters over the years, of course, although it is only after the accepted period of time that we can look back at any of these and dare laugh. At the time of each incident Mother or Father or both have been so incandescent with rage that no one was able to have a good day after all.

Most ingrained in Hopkins Family memory has to be the year Father was dispatched to do his senior-member duties and collect the feted turkey from the obscure farm. The turkey, I might add, had been on order since before it was conceived.

Father returned looking like he had had a double coronary and met his maker. White as a sheet, verging on green, and visibly shaking, he had to inform Mother there was no turkey and the farmer in the arse-end of nowhere denied any knowledge of such an order ever having been placed.

For the Father Figure, that long walk back to the Mothership was the equivalent of the Green Mile, the last steps a man takes before he meets an electrical end on Death Row.

It certainly made the time he came home with a haircut that was 'clearly too short' pale into insignificance in terms of Mother's wrath. (On that fateful day, Dad has really got 'value for money' from the barber, who had reduced his meagre hairline to a mere whisper. He had walked all the way from the garage to the house with a bucket on his head, giving Mother a full five minutes to get herself worked up before she even saw the spectacle of my father's naked head.)

Turns out the turkey farmer had got a bit greedy and, faced with a customer who would pay anything and one turkey left, had sold our bird to someone else.

And so it was that the Family Hopkins was bird-less on Christmas Eve.

A normal family might take this in their stride and go out and buy a couple of chickens. You know, that casual kind of kick that cool families have, where anything goes and it's not a big deal.

Not our family.

The direct link between serving up a morbidly obese pterodactyl and having a good day with peace duly kept, had been severed. Now all bets were off. Mother was wild with rage.

I won't bore you with the details of what unfolded but the outcome was that Mark and I saved the day by going to Tesco and buying a turkey and somehow my mother and I ended up not speaking.

The tension of these moments and the ridiculousness of it all is overwhelming to me at times. I so badly want to be part of one of those families who are super-casual, who rock up laughing with random neighbours or friends and somehow have a glorious day of it. But I suspect such families are an illusion from the telly rather than a reality in most people's life.

I also suspect that these genuinely mad family traits that are hardwired into me and mine are, in fact, different but the same for every family.

What I'm certain of is that as I have grown older, the wish to be abroad or some place else, like a cave with just Lovely Mark and possibly our offspring if they feel inclined to join us, is being replaced by the surety that there are only so many Christmases left with Mum and Dad intact and together in one room. I suspect Father already wonders if this will be his last.

We won't dwell. The memories of Christmases past and the folly and our fear of the Mothership will last long after they (or any of us) are gone. The madness of now will sustain us long into the future so perhaps it is a very worthwhile thing to endure, like an investment in indelibility.

9 December

I think God must be having one of those moments where he looks down and thinks, you know what, that Hopkins bird has put in a good effort this year, I'll give her a little pat on the head. Because Saturday 9 Dec was like a little gift from somewhere sunny.

All my kiddies were home and in a splendid mood and the house felt like a kind of charging point for electric things. Each one of my funny little brood is so entirely different, yet each one was fizzing with a good little energy of their own making.

Golden Balls, my number one and only son, went whizzing off to the local garage where he works as a Saturday boy / cleaner / eager mechanic, returning six hours later looking like a kid that got shoved face-first down a coal mine and used to vacuum up coal dust.

Rather alarmingly for me and my reputation, Max usually returns home from the garage looking as if has deliberately blacked up. Just to add to my fears, he now has the sproutings of a teen moustache, and the oil and dirt he works with gather in these hairs to create a Hitler tache.

It concerns me that one day social services will lurk at the bottom of my road and take pictures of my son whizzing by on an electric bike, sporting black face and a Hitler-tache, and he will be taken into care to protect him from his far-right mother.

But one cannot be a slave to fear, and given my son also has a full blond mullet and is now 6 foot 4, the overall look is more redneck trailer boy than EDL nutter.

My cookie-cutter daughter was back from her caravan and staying home for the weekend, so perfectly positioned to pester Lovely Mark into going out for a mid-morning drink and choosing a Christmas tree together from the local farm shop. Measurements were taken (given last year's tree was overwhelmingly large) and off they went together, like two excitable seal pups on a mission to hunt fish.

And my sensible, majorly autistic-in-a-good-way daughter India (of This Morning name fame) set about creating a timetable in her head for the decorating of the tree.

For her to be okay about the chaos, it has to happen as a family, it has to happen at an agreed time, and she much prefers to be master of one colour of bauble, that she gets to put on the tree in a way she understands. No weird clip-ons or balancing ones or special ones. Just a standard red bauble hung on the tree.

Given the opportunity, she will hang all the same baubles on the same branch, because that makes sense in her mind.

The Hopkins / Cross brigade firmly believes that a tree must be real, it must be massive, and it must be covered in decorations that have been with us since the dawn of time.

There must be our weird paedo angel with bad hair that looks like something out of a Stephen King movie and the sh*t handmade decs that the kids made in school, and it is important that the dodgy squirrel and oversized owl feature.

Only Poppy is allowed to handle the impractical posh decorations Lovely Mark bought in a moment of madness when he forgot he was now a dad of maniacs, as opposed to a cultured single man of wine and fencing.

And I waft about unpacking, facilitating and interfering in equal measure – trying to encourage all the decs into the hands of the young while getting the lights untangled and plug sockets found so all the sparkly stuff can happen.

Lovely Mark is master of lights and beaded garlands: two sets of lights before the decs, bigger lights and beaded garlands after the decs. This process is non-negotiable, and a respectful silence falls as this process is completed because Daddy knows what he is doing. Mum is a maniac. But Dad is not.

On goes the Christmas music, up goes the tree and the lights, and I sit back quietly to enjoy the briefest of unseen moments amid the chaos, and thank my maker or whoever is responsible for this moment, and feel very happy indeed.

How lucky am I? Happy kids, happy house, something that feels splendidly like a very Happy Christmas moment to be part of.

I give Lovely Mark a big kiss and tell him he is perfect.

He tells me to be careful of the extension lead.

This is his love language. You need to be a maniac to understand it.

25 December

The Hopkins family had a good day and keeping the peace went well. The pterodactyl turkey was moist. This moistness is thought to be a 'good thing'.

Rating: 10/10.

Likelihood of staying in parents' will: a solid 8/10.

29 December

The bit after Christmas is just bloody awful for women. No one else really gets it but we totally do.

And the thing is, we aren't supposed to talk about it because if we acknowledge it, it becomes real, and that would be a bloody disaster.

But trying to walk about your own house in which half the occupants are still in full-on do-nothing mode and aren't leaving till after New Year… and you're longing to take down the mountains of decorations, but they're supposed to still be up, AND there are bags of presents and cards and random crap everywhere. It can all feel bizarrely claustrophobic, as if you're silently suffocating in a carbon monoxide haze of your own making.

You know all this shit has to get cleared away and yet none of the other bastards in your family play any real part in keeping things nice; they can't see the problem, nor would they give a shit about it if they could.

Sometimes my excessive and hyper-weird self wants to yell like Captain Caveman on Ketamine, to open the front door, naked, and just start flinging things into the abyss – the bloody cards, the tree, the shitty bag of whatever at the bottom of the stairs, the lights, the dogs, the kids, the crap mugs, the FUCKING BAILEYS…

I just want to lob them all out into the darkness and shout. 'FUCK IT, FUUUUCKKKK ITTTTT. FUUUCCCKKKK YOUUUU ALLL!' at the neighbours.

This feeling only gets bigger as the days tick past. And the more I try and control it, the more it threatens to sneak out the side like a cheeky parp in the pews at a funeral.

It's something to do with inactivity, it's something to do with monotony and idleness, and it's something to do with the terrific effort that's coming next, of clearing it all up, that I find so triggering. And I don't use that word lightly.

Perhaps it is the mundaneness of it.

Perhaps it is the relentlessness of being nice.

Perhaps it is the all-getting-along-so-well, which we are.

I just get that hand-grenade feeling I have known all my life, where the only release is to pull the pin and replace the calm with chaos.

Chaos is my friend. Chaos allows my best self to surge forwards. It feels like home.

In chaos I have purpose: to survive it and to help others survive it also. I take satisfaction in knowing I can do what many others can't. Give me the wild streets of Pretoria and a story to tell, or the rough end of Palestine with something ballsy to do, and I am a superwoman.

Given me the mundane, the monotone or the safe and I want to set my head on fire.

Christmas is a test for my kind. As is much of ordinary life.

30 December

I am not one for endings. And I really don't like goodbyes.

When I am forced in to acknowledging something is over, I agree in advance we won't say goodbye but see you in a little bit. When I am in danger of my little heart breaking I say, 'I WILL see you again' with an emphasis on the WILL.

I sometimes see a flicker of fear in the eyes of the recipient, and I wonder if perhaps I sound a bit like a stalker who plans to creep up on them and lick the windows of their bathroom when they are in the shower.

But I firmly believe that in life our paths cross for a reason and we meet the people we are supposed to; hence we are chatting together here on this page at the end of this year.

Goodness knows, it's been a lot. Big things have happened but I think it's the little stuff of these pages that shows who I really am.

We are all the little stuff of life.

They are our best bits, the things that make us true.

CONCLUSION

People ask me, 'Why are you like this?' gesturing at my small self with genuine curiosity.

I think it's because chaos makes sense to me. I feel at home when I am uncomfortable. I feel at ease when everything is uncertain.

I know I am on some kind of spectrum, and certainly what would now qualify as ADHD, but the answer is never going to be found in a diagnosis or a bottle of something that rattles.

It explains why I am drawn to those living on the periphery of life, homeless or recovering from addiction or seen as odd or bonkers: because they have risked it all to find something different. They aren't trying to show off their way to anyone else. It is just that everyone else's 'normal' is so bizarre to them that they ran full pelt in the opposite direction.

I don't need to explain away being weird and I certainly don't want to be cured.

I think the answer for most of us is to understand why

we are as we are, how that makes us both brilliant and tricky (or, in my case, a liability) all at the same time, and how we best navigate the world and other people using the tools we have.

Our shared aim is to get through this adventure we call life with as much happiness and purpose as we can find.

There are two important things I appreciate as I edge towards 50, a number I never thought I would see:

1   The closer you are to finding your purpose, the happier your life becomes. I think this is most apparent in those who give up a glittering career at the top of their game to pursue the thing they truly love — like the lady who quits being a medical journalist to make cushions. Or those who quit something perceived as prestigious (celebrity, media, fame) to sit quietly and craft jewellery or learn a skill they teach to others.

2   The more you throw yourself at your purpose, the clearer your path becomes. In my life I have found that the more I follow my heart, the more I say yes and react to the call of something inside me, the more clearly I see the way ahead and the more amazing things happen, seemingly by chance, to help me on my way.

Out of nowhere, a chance meeting with someone will present itself, like a plank over a bog, to help me keep going. Or someone who knows about what I am trying to do offers me a hand, or I happen to cross paths with someone with a skill that can amplify my efforts.

This happens time after time, on multiple continents,

when I am applying myself to my path. The greater the risks or sacrifices I make, the more these little angels swoop in to take some of the load.

This is exactly the way I see my audiences on the road during my stand-up tours. The audience are angels, sweeping in to tell me it's okay, it's not all on me, that they just want to be together and feel part of something and I am just a little bit of this whole thing, a little cog in a much bigger machine composed of amazing people. And that makes everything okay.

I know I am shy. I know I am not the thing others imagine I am or I sometimes pretend to be. But I also know all the different bits of me combine to make it okay, to keep me on my path.

If you think all of this is just psychobabble, the rantings of a mad woman trying to make herself feel better or excuse away some of her disgraceful behaviour, you may be right.

But what if my way of understanding the world is true?

What if the point of life is as simple as: to find your purpose. And what if the closer you get to your purpose the happier you become, and the more you dedicate yourself to finding your purpose, the more amazing angels appear, sweeping you up and carrying you along with them towards a better way of living.

That's what I believe as I head towards 50. And that's what I encourage everyone I meet to feel.

Cut yourself free from rules, possessions, fraudulent emotions imposed by others (guilt, shame). Turn down the volume on people who are irrelevant to your happiness.

I can guarantee things will be okay. I can look you in the eye and tell you: you are doing great, you can do this, and you are going to make it – because all you have to do is keep going for one more day.

And when you find yourself feeling happy for a moment, perhaps feeling something close to content, it's a sign that you are walking your path.

Listen to yourself, support yourself, preserve yourself.

I CAN. I AM. I WILL. To yourself be true.